THE EPIC OF
ASKIA
MOHAMMED

African Epic Series
THOMAS A. HALE AND JOHN W. JOHNSON, GENERAL EDITORS

Jeseré Nouhou Malio on left recounting *The Epic of Askia Mohammed*,
accompanied by Soumana Abdou playing the three-stringed molo,
in Saga, Niger, December 30, 1980. Photo by Thomas A. Hale

THE EPIC OF

ASKIA MOHAMMED

Recorded, Translated,
Edited, and Annotated by
Thomas A. Hale

Recounted by
Nouhou Malio

With the assistance of
Mounkaila Maiga, Fatima Mounkaila,
Abdoulaye Dan Louma, Moussa Djibo,
and Ousmane Tandina

Performance accompanied by Soumana Abdou

INDIANA UNIVERSITY PRESS

Bloomington and Indianapolis

This book is a publication of

Indiana University Press
601 North Morton Street
Bloomington, IN 47404-3797 USA

http://iupress.indiana.edu

Telephone orders 800-842-6796
Fax orders 812-855-7931
Orders by e-mail iuporder@indiana.edu

Library of Congress Cataloging-in-Publication Data

Mamar Kassaye deeda. English & Songhai.
    The epic of Askia Mohammed / recorded, translated, edited, and
annotated by Thomas A. Hale ; recounted by Nouhou Malio with the
assistance of Mounkaila Maiga . . . [et al.].
        p.   cm.—(African epic series)
    Includes bibliographical references and index.
    Translation from Songhay.
    ISBN 0-253-32926-4 (cl : alk. paper).—ISBN 0-253-20990-0 (pbk. :
alk. paper)
        1. Mohammed I, Askia of Songhai, 1443?–1538—In literature.
    2. Epic poetry, Songhai—Translations—History and criticism.
    3. Songhai (African people)—Folklore. I. Hale, Thomas A.
    II. Malio, Nouhou, d. 1986. III. Maiga, Mounkaila. IV. Title.
    V. Series.
PL8685.9.M36E5   1996
896'.5—dc20   95-21699

2 3 4 5 6 06 05 04 03 02 01

CONTENTS

PREFACE

The Epic of Askia Mohammed recounts the life of the most famous ruler of the Songhay empire, a man who reigned in Gao, an old city in present-day eastern Mali, from 1493 to 1528. The text presented here, 1,602 lines long, is the first linear translation of the epic from the region south of Gao that became the Songhay heartland after the fall of the empire in 1591. The epic was narrated by Nouhou Malio during two evenings in Saga, a small town on the Niger River just two miles downstream from Niamey, the capital of Niger. As with the first volume in this series, *The Epic of Son-Jara* translated by John William Johnson and a team of Malian scholars, this text has not been reconstructed or rewritten by editors. It is a word-for-word translation of a narrative recorded from an oral performance by a griot, or *jeseré*. The introduction to the epic and the annotations that follow it will provide the necessary context for understanding the extraordinary life of Askia Mohammed as portrayed today by modern artisans of the word.

This version of the epic first appeared in a bilingual Songhay-English format as the appendix to a much longer comparative study, *Scribe, Griot, and Novelist: Narrative Interpreters of the Songhay Empire*. My goal in that book was to see what three different kinds of narrators of the Songhay past had to say to each other and to scholars in different fields who might not normally see the connections for many years. The texts included the *Tarîkh el-Fettâch* and the *Tarîkh es-Sudan*, eight hundred pages of written chronicles from the Timbuktu region, dating from the sixteenth and seventeenth centuries, the recently recorded *Epic of Askia Mohammed*, and *Le Devoir de violence*, a modern African novel in French by Malian author Yambo Ouologuem. It won great acclaim in France after publication in 1968 but also generated considerable controversy over the novelist's use of a variety of sources, historical and fictional.

The purpose here is more modest—to provide a readable introduction to the epic text alone. But the results of the comparison carried out in *Scribe, Griot, and Novelist* will help considerably to contextualize the oral narrative. As with *Son-Jara*, the goal is to make available to the public another example of African epic from an authentic source in a format that conveys as much as possible the aura of the original performance. Instructors in courses on epic, African literature, African history, folklore, and anthropology will find that the narrative provides a wide range of insights into the ways an African people hear their past across a gulf of five centuries.

The epic was recorded on the evenings of December 30, 1980, and January 26, 1981, in Saga, Niger, on a UHER Report 4000, a five-inch reel-to-reel tape recorder. The first session lasted for several hours, beginning with the Zarma epic of Mali Bero and continuing with the first half of Askia Mohammed. The second session lasted about one hour. Total time for the epic was approximately one and one-half hours. The long delay between the two performances was due to the illness of Nouhou Malio.

The original tapes are on deposit at the Archives of Traditional Music at Indiana University. Cassette copies are also stored at the Institute for Research in Social Sciences of Abdou Moumouni University of Niamey, Niger, as well as with the families of the late Nouhou Malio and Soumana Abdou, his accompanist on the three-stringed *molo*, a lute-like instrument.

Although I am responsible for recording this version of the epic, as well as many others by different bards, numerous scholars contributed to the ten-year task of transcribing, translating, and annotating *The Epic of Askia Mohammed*. Readers who may wonder why there are so many undecipherable lines in the epic will understand better some of the problems by reading the lengthy itinerary that the text has taken from those two evenings in Saga to the printed page in 1990.

At Abdou Moumouni University of Niamey, Mounkaila Seydou Boulhassane Maïga, a translator and transcriber in the Lexicography Laboratory of the Linguistics Department, carried out a rapid first transcription and translation from the original Songhay recording. Then a working group of scholars and students at the university that included Fatima Mounkaila, Abdoulaye Dan Louma, Djibo Moussa, and me focused on the translation at weekly meetings for the remainder of the 1980–81 academic year.

After several years of some rather complex word processing at Penn State that required the setting up of four lines for each line of text (the original Songhay, a word-for-word French translation, a more literate French translation, and an English translation), I returned to Niger in 1987 for further analysis of the narrative. Djibo Moussa listened to the original recording and found that 20 percent of the lines had not been transcribed and translated earlier because they were in archaic Soninké, the occult language of the Songhay, and perhaps other languages.

In 1988 Ousmane Mahamane Tandina visited Penn State to assist me on the transcription and translation of many of these lines. In 1989, I returned to Niger again for a reading of the text by the dean of Niger's scholars in oral literature, Diouldé Laya. He found additional items that needed interpretation and confirmed the great significance of this version. As the epic was about to go to press in the fall of 1989, Fatima Mounkaila helped to refine the translation during a visit to Penn State. More recently, in spring 1994, Aissata Sidikou, Salifou Siddo, and Boubacar Assoumi, Nigérien graduate students at Penn State, have offered additional revisions to the translation. This epic, then, illustrates one of my conclusions in *Scribe, Griot and Novelist*: all texts, written and oral, are dynamic, not static, because they are subject to correction, rereading, and reinterpretation.

In *Scribe, Griot, and Novelist*, I thanked the many people who contributed to the processing of the recording and the comparisons made with the other two forms of narrative. I want to reiterate my appreciation of those who played the most important roles in helping me to advance the epic from tape to print: *jeserédunka*, or master griot, Nouhou Malio, who was willing to share his knowledge so that others outside Niger could learn more about the Songhay past; Soumana Abdou, his accompanist, who has served as a most cordial and helpful contact person for me in Saga in the years since the recording; Ousmane Mahamane Tandina, Fatima Mounkaila, Djibo Moussa, and Abdoulaye Harouna, all of whom assisted at different stages in the processing of the text; Diouldé Laya, Director of the Center for the Study of Linguistics and History by Oral Traditions in Niamey, whose unflagging encouragement of scholars working in Niger has contributed significantly to greater understanding of the cultural heritage of the country.

The following institutions supported the task of recording the performance and the subsequent work of processing the text: the

Fulbright-Hays Program and the University Affiliation Grant Program administered by the United States Information Agency; the Faculty of Letters and Social Sciences of the University of Niamey; and the Institute for the Arts and Humanistic Studies and the College of the Liberal Arts of The Pennsylvania State University.

GENEALOGY

The genealogy of the Askias in the epic is much less complex than that in the Timbuktu chronicles, not only because of the great time span between events five hundred years ago and the present but also because the griots are more interested in the stories of those who, they believe, made a mark in history. They generally omit undistinguished rulers who lasted for only a few years and accomplished little.

Below is a short version of the genealogy of main characters in the epic. The reader needs to keep in mind that it represents a compressed form of history. For example, we know that Sonni Ali Ber was not the uncle of Askia Mohammed. He was, instead, a ruler who died on the way home from a military campaign. Askia Mohammed actually challenged one of Sonni Ali Ber's descendants for the throne. Also the identity of some of the descendants of Askia Mohammed as listed by the *jeseré* does not match clearly the very precise genealogies of the Timbuktu chroniclers.

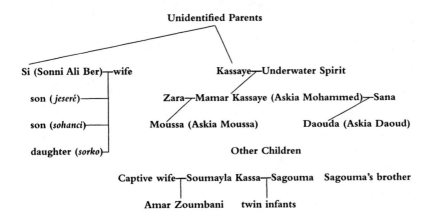

THE EPIC OF
ASKIA
MOHAMMED

Introduction

The diverse peoples of the Sahel and Savanna regions of West Africa share a common cultural history in the great empires that rose and fell during the last thousand years: Ghana, Mali, and Songhay. The Songhay empire absorbed much of the earlier Mali empire during the fifteenth- and sixteenth-century reign of Askia Mohammed. Given the proximity in time and space of these two great political entities as well as the common features of the griot profession across the Sahel and Savanna regions, it is not surprising to find numerous parallels in both form and function between *The Epic of Son-Jara* and *The Epic of Askia Mohammed*. But there are also many differences.

THE HERO

A major distinction emerges immediately in the historicity of the hero. In the Introduction to *Son-Jara*, John William Johnson remarked that it is much easier to know what the hero of the Mali empire represents today than to understand who he may have been 750 years ago. For Askia Mohammed, however, contemporary chroniclers from Timbuktu have left us detailed written records of his rise to power, his reign from 1493 to 1528, his pilgrimage to Mecca around the years 1497–98, the slow decline of the empire after his overthrow by his son Askia Moussa in 1528, and the empire's destruction in 1591 by an invading army from Morocco. That record, of course, differs in many ways from the narrative recounted by Nouhou Malio in 1980–81. The comparison between the two texts reveals much not only about the hero but also about how the Songhay view the past today and how their values are reflected in the dialogue over five centuries between the two different kinds of narratives.

Askia Mohammed was not the only leader to be inscribed in the history of the Songhay empire. For many reasons, however, he is the most famous. First, the empire reached its apogee during his reign. For generations Songhay had existed as a political entity on the banks of the Niger approximately half way between the present-day cities of Timbuktu in Mali and Niamey in Niger. But it developed as a significant political force in the region thanks to the rise of another leader, Sonni Ali Ber, beginning in 1463, about the time that Mali's influence in West Africa began to wane. Sonni Ali Ber aggressively expanded the zone of Songhay influence, and by the time of his death in 1492, he had laid the foundations for a state that Askia Mohammed was to develop even further with a complex system of administration, a well-equipped army and navy, and a network of large government-owned farms.

Another reason for the respect and admiration shown Askia Mohammed during his time and by subsequent generations was his piety. Since much of what we know about him was recorded by Islamic scribes, the image of the ruler, both in the chronicles and to some extent in the oral tradition, is colored by a highly positive view of a man who did much for Islam in West Africa. He demonstrated great respect for the keepers of the Islamic faith in the region, especially its most learned scholars in Timbuktu, launched wars to spread Islam to those who did not believe in the religion, exchanged correspondence with Moslem theologians in North Africa, and, finally, made a much-heralded pilgrimage to Mecca.

The scribes draw a sharp contrast between his behavior and that of Sonni Ali Ber, who is reputed to have ordered the burning of Timbuktu in 1468 and the killing of thirty virgin daughters of the city's religious leaders. Although it is not entirely evident that Sonni Ali Ber was as evil as he is portrayed, nor that Askia Mohammed was as good as the chroniclers describe him, the Songhay ruler's reputation has certainly benefited from the contrast with his predecessor during the last five centuries.

Finally, Askia Mohammed appears as the greatest of Songhay rulers because those who followed him, his sons, and grandsons, were relatively ineffective—with the exception of Askia Daoud—at governing the state he had so carefully built. In fact, the scribes explain the defeat of the Songhay army at the hands of Moroccan-led invaders as the inevitable result of decadence that set in as the empire declined, especially during the years just prior to 1591.

THE GRIOT

Before discussing the person who narrated this epic, it is useful to explain the complex nature of the word *griot*. It is a regional term that dates to the early seventeenth century. Its origin remains unclear. There are many theories—more than a dozen—but no convincing evidence—to account for its roots in Berber, Arabic, Wolof, Portuguese, French, and Spanish. The current form of the word comes to us via French and has spread from the Sahel and Savanna regions, where it often takes on negative connotations, to Europe, North America, and the Caribbean, where, among people of the African diaspora, it has come to serve as a powerful symbol of their cultural heritage. But each people in the vast horizontal swath of West Africa where griots live has its own term or terms for different types of these wordsmiths. In the epic, I have translated the Songhay word *jeseré* as *griot*. But in this introduction, when referring to griots in a particular context, I will use the local term, *jeseré* in Songhay and *jeli* in Maninka. When discussing griots in a broader context, for example Niger, where there are several different peoples and languages, *griot, wordsmith, bard,* or *artisan of the word* will convey the regional nature of the profession.

As with the *jeli* who chants *The Epic of Son-Jara* and other narratives about heroes of the Mali empire, the *jeseré* who recounts the story of Askia Mohammed is a member of what is often called a caste that holds a functional monopoly over the use of certain kinds of speech. The term *caste*, however, does not fit very well because it implies hierarchy. As Johnson notes, griots do not fit into a social hierarchy. It is important to add, nevertheless, that they are often described as inferior by some people in their own society, especially those of noble origin. Blacksmiths, griots, weavers, and woodcarvers may be viewed more appropriately as belonging to hereditary guilds or unions. They see themselves as distinct from other groups in society, not necessarily of higher or lower status, as is the case for those of noble or captive origin. The fact that a noble would not consider marriage with someone of griot origin reflects to a large extent this fundamental difference as well as a very complex social relationship that ties the griot to those who are the subjects of his or her verbal art. It is a relationship that scholars are only beginning to understand.

The Mande term *nyamakala*, "possessor of occult power," designates all those who come from these specialist groups, and it occurs also among the Songhay. But in western Niger *nyamakala* is simply a generic word for *jeseré* or griot. Although it is not evident that the Songhay *jeseré* is, like his Malian counterpart, a member of a certain clan known to specialize in the oral tradition, it is clear that some Songhay clan names associated with nobility, for example the Maiga who claim descent from Askia Mohammed, do not normally appear among those who fulfill the functions of the *jeseré*.

One other link between the Mande and Songhay worlds reveals much about the deep cultural roots of the region. The Soninké people descended from the ancient Ghana empire, which preceded the Mali empire, use the term *geseré* to designate a griot. Soninké is a Mande language. Askia Mohammed of the Touré clan appears to have come from Soninké ancestors. Traditionally, the Songhay oral tradition was maintained in Soninké. In *Scribe, Griot, and Novelist*, I have suggested that the use of Soninké is probably the result of an influx of Soninké *geseru* to Gao after Askia Mohammed Touré came to power. Today, one version of Soninké survives in the Songhay world in a few small and isolated communities. A slightly different version also serves as the occult language of the *jeseré* as well as of traditional healers and sorcerers. It is this occult language, only partially decipherable today by modern Soninké speakers, that accounts for the large number of untranslated lines in the epic. Where this form of Soninké is understandable, I have underlined the translation to highlight its use.

The functions of the Songhay *jeseré* closely parallel those of his Mande counterpart. The *jeseré* is a historian and chronicler who recounts history both for the general public and more particularly for those noble families whose ancestors are actors in the events of the past. Entertainment is another important function. One may hear a Songhay *jeseré* listing genealogies, recounting the past, and playing the three-stringed *molo*, a close cousin to the Mande *ngoni*, at weddings, installations of chiefs, and naming ceremonies. Another role is that of articulating appropriate behavior, whether for a chief or for a bride at a wedding. For example, in the video "Griottes of Sahel: Female Keepers of the Songhay Oral Tradition in Niger," a female griot (*jeseré weyboro*), Weybi Karma, sings a warning to a young bride that if she is abused by anyone in her new family, it is no crime for her to leave the house.

Service as a mediator in disputes and delicate negotiations is another function of the Songhay *jeseré* in the Sahel and Savanna regions. The role of the griot as advisor to rulers that Johnson identifies among Mande *jelilu*, or griots, also occurs in the Songhay world although, as he points out, it is easier to discern this function in the context of an epic than in modern society where presidents are surrounded by ministers. In *The Epic of Askia Mohammed*, when the ruler crosses the Red Sea to complete the pilgrimage to Mecca, only two of his followers remain in his entourage: his Moslem advisor and his *jeseré*.

Other changes that Johnson notes for Mande *jelilu* occur also for their Songhay neighbors as well as for griots throughout the region—diminished patronage from noble families, increased support from merchants and others who have acquired wealth, and a certain amount of employment by the government. For a variety of reasons some griots have become local institutions, representing either a village, town, or region. In Niger, for example, griots have performed at state functions and on occasion accompanied the president of the country on official trips. Producers of radio and television programs rely on griots and griottes as well as on other traditional entertainers and performers to balance the airtime of offerings in the eight national languages of Niger. In Mali, Niger, and other countries of the Sahel and Savanna regions, portraits of the most famous griots have appeared on stamps. As in Mali and other countries, the griots of Niger are now traveling more widely, not simply around the country but to expatriate communities on the coast, especially in Abidjan, Accra, Lomé, and Cotonou during the season between the fall harvest and the early summer rains. Songhay wordsmiths have not yet followed the path of their Mande colleagues, some of whom have moved from a regional to a global stage by appearing at concert halls and university auditoriums in Europe, North America, and Asia. But it is likely that a few of the most famous of them—for example Djeliba Badié, the most sought after *jeseré* in Niamey, Niger—will soon be heard outside the African continent.

NOUHOU MALIO

I recorded narratives from nearly two dozen griots in a 40,000-square-mile region of Western Niger in 1980–81 while serving as a Fulbright senior lecturer in African literature and American civilization at the University of Niamey. But for many reasons rooted in the changing economic and demographic conditions of the country, I found that a large number of the most talented and experienced griots live in the capital of Niger, Niamey. When I was introduced to them, I always asked who their teachers were. Often, an urban griot referred me to Nouhou Malio, a *jeserédunka* who lived just outside the city.

When I interviewed Nouhou Malio on January 26, 1981, he reported that he was sixty-five years old, and that he and his brother Maliki had inherited the profession from their ancestors. They learned first from their father, who died before Nouhou reached maturity. Nouhou then continued his studies with his older brother, who died around 1960.

Nouhou Malio described the training of a griot as an endless process that began around a fire in the evening with seven-year-old children contributing millet stalks and wood to keep the blaze going. They prepared in accordance with a method that matched the learning of the Koran. Three names in a genealogy were memorized each night. Children of griots required special attention if they were to succeed in the profession. In order to inculcate facility in verbal art, explained Nouhou Malio, one needed to wash the newborn child in water that had been taken from several different houses and then boiled. Pupils from outside the griot's family, normally from families of related groups such as leatherworkers or blacksmiths, paid their way by helping the master griot in the fields. After several years, these apprentices would go off to learn from other wordsmiths.

Nouhou Malio is of Songhay origin but he lived in a suburb of a cosmopolitan capital that includes people from all ethnic groups in the country, especially the Zarma, Songhay, Hausa, and Peul. He recounted much of the epic in the Zarma dialect, a variant of Songhay that the Zarma consider to be a distinct language. By tradition, the Zarma do not have griots, and so they must rely upon the Songhay for the functions carried out by these artisans of the word.

Nouhou Malio appeared to be a modest man who did not seek attention. He said that he had never performed on the radio, and he added that he did not travel very much. When I returned to see him four months after our recording sessions, his neighbors reported that he had left for his farm fifteen miles away and would not return until the end of the agricultural season. When I came back the next time, in 1987, I learned from Soumana Abdou that Nouhou Malio had died the preceding year.

THE TEXT

As Johnson points out in his discussion of *Son-Jara*, there is some debate over whether one can define any genre, epic or otherwise, as a universal form or instead as what he has termed "an ethno-aesthetic" construct definable only by its users. In Songhay the word for the kind of long narrative that we call epic is simply *deeda*, or long narrative. The distinction between literature and history for many Songhay listeners is not always clear-cut. But if we place *The Epic of Askia Mohammed* in the broader context of the West African epic, many common features emerge that allow us to identify this narrative as an epic.

Poetic Qualities

In the Mande epic of *Son-Jara*, Johnson lists three modes employed by the griot to tell the story: narrative, praise-proverb, and song. The first two of these modes appear also in this version of *The Epic of Askia Mohammed*. Much of the epic is in the narrative mode. But Nouhou Malio takes pains to vary the telling of events by the use of dialogue and shifts from third person to first person, especially in the scene where Askia Mohammed kills his uncle and then assumes power. The effect there is to bring the reader into the past as a witness, along with the griot who exclaims on line 178, "Did you see him!" At other times, the distinction between the narrator and the events is deliberately blurred—we don't know if the *jeseré* is speaking or a character. Sometimes Nouhou Malio appears to slip into a form of free indirect discourse that, again, brings the listener closer to the action. At two highly significant points he figuratively turns directly to the audience to ask if listeners have understood an important lesson: first at the beginning of the epic, at lines 214–18, where he explains the origin of the *jeseré* in a series of mini etiological tales, and later, toward the end, at line 1402, where in a dialogue between Amar Zoumbani and his father we are given a very pointed lesson about the social hierarchy in the Sahel region.

Other devices that underscore the poetic nature of the text include frequent repetition of words and entire lines for emphasis or to indicate the passage of time (101–103, 173), metonymy to emphasize a subject's qualities (the description of cavalry as simply horses), and comparisons to show how an action takes place (406–408 where the flight of the *sohanci* is compared with an airplane and a hawk). The griot reserves the device of the metaphor for praise-proverb sections where he seeks to convey in a more symbolic manner the extraordinary character of a leader, either evil (Askia Moussa, 482–489) or good (Askia Daoud, 507–590).

The recounting of genealogies in the epic takes on a particularly poetic quality because of the alternation between the archaic Soninké (underlined) and the Songhay in listing names, especially after the verb "to father"—*sara* in Soninké and hay in Songhay. "A *sara* . . . A hay" (He *fathered* . . . He fathered). It is during the recitation of genealogies in these two languages that one senses not only the poetic nature of the epic but also its very deep cultural roots.

Only once during the performance did Nouhou Malio employ gesture. Sitting beneath an electric light in a steel and plastic patio chair in the main room of a relative's home, he lowered his hands in a scooping motion to the concrete floor to describe the actions of Askia Mohammed at the tomb of the Prophet Mohammed. At other times, he relied on ideophones, sounds that illustrate action, to convey movement: 1002, *jip* (zip) for the sound of jumping off a horse, and 1038, *urufo* (whoops) for the sound of falling into a hole.

Structure and Narrative Style

As with the *Son-Jara, Askia Mohammed* is made up of episodes composed of themes that themselves are made up of small components such as genealogies, praise-names, proverbs, ideophones, and other rhetorical devices. The episodes are defined to a large extent by their location. The opening scene is in Gao, the capital, on the left bank of the Niger River (1–269). The scene then shifts to the campaign trail, with a brief reference to the Mossi people to the southwest of Gao in Burkina Faso before ending up in Mecca and Medina in Saudia Arabia (270–375). The episode of the battle against the Bargantché in northern Benin (376–480) constitutes a separate chapter in his campaign to conquer other people. Here the *jeseré* shifts to the ruler's descendants in a confusing and symbolic series of genealogies that lasts from 481 to 803. Two episodes involving considerable compression of history then follow. The first is the long story of Soumayla Kassa, symbol of Songhay resistance in Gao against the Arma, the Songhay term for the invaders, in the years following 1591 when the region was ruled by a Moroccan governor, or pasha, from headquarters in Timbuktu (804 to 1456). The second episode brings together the Zarma and Songhay people as Mali Bero and his nephew Yefarma Issaka, legendary leaders of the Zarma, become involved in the defensive battle against the Moroccans (1457 to 1602).

These episodes, however, are not clearly defined in the text. Nouhou Malio shifted from one to the next without ceremony. Although he sometimes paused briefly or slowed down, especially in passages where there was much parellelism, the flow of the narrative was continuous, broken only by the long hiatus of several weeks for his illness.

Heroic Content

The hero in *The Epic of Askia Mohammed*, like his counterpart in the Mande and in so many other epics in other parts of the world, must overcome extreme adversity as a child. When he kills his domineering uncle, however, his destiny as a hero instantly becomes evident to the people around him. But like Son-Jara, he cannot rely simply on his strength and wit to succeed. For the Songhay as well as for the Mande peoples, magic plays an important role at critical junctures in life. For example, Askia Mohammed was fathered by a spirit who lived in a world under the Niger River. Later, as ruler he cannot escape from near-defeat at the hands of the Bargantché without resorting to the supernatural abilities of his sorcerer, who flies through the air like Superman to reach the leader's mother five hundred miles away, and then returns with three magical devices from her. As with Son-Jara, each event—birth, conquering his uncle, battling his neighbors, and making the pilgrimage to Mecca—serves to transform the hero as he, in turn, transforms and expands the empire he controls.

Multigeneric Qualities

As with the Mande epics, parts of the Songhay epic can be broken up into different genres, ranging from descriptive narrations of events to long genealogies, praise-poems about individuals, brief etiological tales, and proverbs. Some of these components of the epic, for example the genealogies, are often recited independently of the epic. Johnson affirms that this "multigeneric structure is an important defining characteristic of this form of oral folklore," a statement that fits as well with what we know about the Songhay epic.

Legendary Belief Structure

Although Askia Mohammed is a well documented ruler, like Son-Jara his character and life have been shaped in the epic to fit a certain ideal or pattern. In this sense, we can say that he is a legendary hero, one who is much larger in many ways than the historical person on whom he is based.

Multifunctionality

The epic not only provides entertainment at important events but also serves to remind people of the finer distinctions that demarcate different groups in society—as in the case of Amar Zoumbani, son of a king and a slave. As with Son-Jara, we find many other groups appearing on the stage, often announced by etiological tales: the *jeseré*, the *sohanci* (sorcerer), the *sorko* (praise-singer of spirits from the river), the captive, the warrior, the holy man. Johnson's observation "that bards tend to describe society as they believe it ought to be rather than as it may actually be" certainly fits here (11).

Transmission of Culture

As in the Mande world, the Songhay epic constitutes a catalog of Songhay society, with weapons, boats, utensils, traps, musical instruments, foods, clothing, animals, spirits, and items of magic all mentioned or described. Johnson suggests that the extent of this cultural information may be one measure of a griot's reputation (11). If the epic, he explains, is the mirror of society and is used to enculturate the audience, then the griot who competes with other bards may want to include as much of these diverse kinds of information as possible.

History

An important feature of the epic is the way history is transformed and telescoped. A common feature of the epic is what Joseph Miller terms "the hourglass effect." The narrative places great emphasis on the beginning and ending events of the story, but not much on the middle. The comparison of Nouhou Malio's version of the past with that of the chroniclers reveals that many of the less-successful leaders of the Songhay empire who followed Askia Moussa did not merit much attention from the *jeseré*. Askia Moussa, the son who deposed his father and then exiled him to an island in the Niger River, appears only briefly, and then only in a symbolic language that emphasizes the man's power. Askia Daoud, the most often praised of Askia Mohammed's sons, is well known for killing two lions to demonstrate his claim to the Songhay throne. Other rulers disappear in a blur of genealogies that will leave the reader rather confused.

The narrative appears to have two parts: the first is that of the life of Askia Mohammed, and the second that of Soumayla Kassa and Amar Zoumbani. The link between the two is the story of Askia Daoud plus the symbolic references to Askia Moussa and some other leaders. The story of Soumayla Kassa and Amar Zoumbani, however, suggests a major compression of history because it contains an account of a siege of the city of Gao. It is fairly evident now that Nouhou Malio and other keepers of the oral tradition have conflated the resistance of the Songhay against the invading Moroccans in 1591 with a revolt of the city several generations later when Moroccan power in the region began to fade.

A more significant difference between the record of the past conveyed by the chroniclers and that which we find in the epic, however, appears in the reasons given for the fall of the empire. Where the Moslem chroniclers describe the fall as the result of social decadence (incest, adultery, etc.), the *jeseré* implies that the Songhay defeat comes from a more fundamental social weakness, a failure to observe the basic social rules that control the separation of society's different classes of people. The story of Amar Zoumbani, Sagouma, and the fall of Gao illustrates the kind of behavior that goes against the rules and seems to lead inevitably to disaster.

Belief

If the epic describes the past, the traditions that emerge from it are still important for listeners in the present. The Islamic values conveyed in the chronicles are not lacking in the epic, but what complements them is a belief system that continues to flourish today. One need only read the works of anthropologist Paul Stoller to understand why the title of the epic in the original Songhay is not "Askia Mohammed Deeda" but "Mamar Kassaye Deeda," Mamar, diminutive of Mohammed, son of Kassaye. She is a woman endowed with great magical powers. Today a woman by the same name or title reigns in Wanzerbé as the most powerful sorceress of the region. The belief in sorcery, traditional healing, and other spiritual forms continues to hold great value for many Songhay as evidenced by Stoller's research as well as by that of other scholars. The epic serves as a catalog of this belief system, from the magical devices Askia Mohammed's mother sends him to help him escape from the difficult battle against the Bargantché to the charms that protected the city of Gao from the bullets of the Moroccan-led soldiers.

Résumé of the Plot

Although *The Epic of Askia Mohammed* is somewhat shorter than *The Epic of Son-Jara*, it may seem equally confusing both because of the oral nature of the narrative and because the *jeseré* shifts without transition from one episode to the next. Line numbers listed below mark the different themes.

Line Theme

1 Story of how Kassaye's children are all put to death by her brother Si (Sonni Ali Ber), because of a prophecy that one of them will kill him.

23 Spirit from under the river visits Kassaye, proposes solution to her problem.

41 Kassaye becomes pregnant.

44 Bargantché servant becomes pregnant.

48 Kassaye gives birth to Mamar, gives infant to her servant.

54 Servant gives birth to a daughter, gives infant to Kassaye.

63 Si orders killing of daughter, thinking it is Kassaye's child.

70 Mamar is named.

82 Mamar crawls on feet, pulls beard of Si, who is suspicious of him.

97 Kassaye gives Mamar to Si to become his groom.

108 Mamar suffers insults of other children who say he has no father.

121 Mamar's father comes to give Kassaye a ring that will enable Mamar to see him.

148 Mamar sees his father at the river and receives a stallion, lances, a saber, and a shield.

185 Mamar kills his uncle Si at the prayer ground and assumes chieftaincy.

209 His cousin, son of Si, sings his praises and becomes the first *jeseré*, or griot.

219 His other cousin, second son of Si, becomes a *sohanci* a kind of sorcerer.

225 His third cousin, the daughter of Si, becomes a *sorko*, praise-singer of spirits from the river.

882 Sagouma discovers that her brother is very unhappy about the generosity and success of Amar Zoumbani in courting the rich woman.

890 Sagouma suggests that her brother demonstrate his generosity by giving Amar, son of a family captive, to the griots who sing the praises of generous suitors.

902 Sagouma's brother does so the next day, causing concern among the people and upsetting Amar, who doesn't understand his ambiguous social status.

907 Amar asks his father, Soumayla Kassa, about the situation.

910 Soumayla Kassa explains why Amar is of captive origin.

918 For the feast of Tabaski, Amar demands a black stallion similar tò that owned by the brother of Sagouma.

932 Soumayla Kassa sends men to find such a horse, but they can only locate one with some white markings, which they cover with dye.

978 Amar goes to the prayer ground, seeking a fight with Sagouma's brother, but does not find him there.

992 On the return home, Amar's clothes become stained with dye from the horse.

1004 Amar cuts the tendons on the horse's legs, then goes home to cry.

1017 Soumayla Kassa decides to console his son by setting a trap for Sagouma's brother.

1038 Sagouma's brother comes to Soumayla Kassa's house, falls into the trap, and is smothered by dirt.

1047 Sagouma's servant witnesses the murder and reports it to Sagouma.

1079 Sagouma kills her twin sons and leaves Gao to find a man from among the Moroccan-led occupiers who will kill Soumayla Kassa and Amar Zoumbani.

1156 A man named Bayero agrees to undertake a war against Gao.

1176 Men, weapons, and supplies are now sent downriver to ready for the attack.

1203 Women play a key role in supplying the army.

1213 Bayero's army begins a seven-month siege of Gao, a city protected by a python, an ox, and a hen.

1274 A woman from Gao reveals the secret of the levitating city to an enemy soldier.

1289 The attackers fire into the air and succeed in destroying Gao. The defenders retreat downriver, fighting a rearguard action.

1359 Soumayla Kassa hears Sagouma playing the *godji*, a one-stringed violin, for an enemy soldier. He kills the man.

1390 Amar Zoumbani spots a jar of waste water used for washing millet and suggests that his thirsty father drink it. His father replies that the suggestion is a sign of Amar's captive origin.

1438 Amar violates tradition about sleeping with local women and dismounting horses in the morning, acts perceived as bringing bad luck to the retreating Songhay army.

1457 Mali Bero, leader of the neighboring Zarma people, joins the war on the side of the Songhay resistance.

1464 Zarma leaders and seers agree that if they enter the war, Mali Bero's nephew Yefarma Issaka will want to participate, and he will die.

1482 Mali Bero sends Yefarma on a mission to the Foga region in the east to prevent him from getting involved in the war.

1499 Yefarma meets a woman who reveals the truth about his mission.

1540 A horse reveals to a Fulani seer that Yefarma is returning and that he will die.

1544 Yefarma returns to complain about being kept out of the war.

1586 Yefarma is killed by an enemy arrow near Boubon, upriver from Niamey.

The Epic

1 Mamar Kassaye, didn't the Songhay people narrate it to you?
2 Mamar Kassaye himself whom they talk about.
3 Mamar himself, the son of Kassaye.
4 This Kassaye, it is Si who is her brother.
5 Si and Kassaye, they have the same mother and the same father.
6 Kassaye is the woman.
7 It is Si who is the man, it is he who is on the throne, it is he who is the chief.
8 Kassaye is his sister, she is in his compound.
9 Any husband who marries Kassaye, and if she gives birth,
10 The seers have said "Listen"—they told Si it is Kassaye who will give birth to a child who will kill him and take over the throne of Gao.
11 It is Kassaye who will give birth to a child.
12 That child will kill Si and will take the position of ruler.
13 Si also heard about this.
14 All the children that Kassaye gave birth to,
15 As soon as Kassaye delivered it, Si killed it.
16 Every child that Kassaye delivered, as soon as it was born, Si killed it.
17 Until she had given birth to seven children,
18 Which her brother Si killed.
19 Kassaye had enough, she said she would no longer take a husband.
20 She stayed like that.
21 Si is on his throne,
22 While Kassaye remained like that.

23 Until, until, until, until one day, much later, in the middle of the
    night,
24 A man came who was wearing beautiful clothes.
25 He was a real man, he was tall, someone who looked good in
    white clothes, his clothes were really beautiful.
26 One could smell perfume everywhere.
27 He came in to sit down next to Kassaye.
28 They chatted with each other, they chatted, they chatted.
29 He said to her, "It is really true.
30 "Kassaye, I would like to make love with you.
31 "Once we make love together,
32 "You will give birth to a boy,
33 "Whom Si will not be able to kill.
34 "It is he who will kill Si and will become the ruler."
35 Kassaye said to him, "What?"
36 He said, "By Allah."
37 She said, "Good, in the name of Allah."
38 Each night the man came.
39 It is during the late hours that he came.
40 Each time during the coolness of the late evening.
41 Until Kassaye became pregnant by him.
42 Kassaye carried her pregnancy.
43 Kassaye had a Bargantché captive.
44 It is the Bargantché woman who is her captive, she lives in her
    house, and she too is pregnant.
45 They remained like that.
46 Kassaye kneeled down to give birth.
47 The captive kneeled down to give birth.
48 So Kassaye, Kassaye gave birth to a boy.
49 The captive gave birth to a girl.
50 Then Kassaye took the daughter of the captive, she took her
    home with her.
51 She took her son and gave it to the captive.
52 So the people left for the palace.
53 They said to Si:
54 "The Bargantché captive has given birth."
55 He said, "What did she get?"
56 They said, "A boy."

57 He said, "May Allah be praised, may our Lord give him a long life and may he be useful."

58 Then they were thoughtful for a moment.

59 They got up and informed him that Kassaye had given birth.

60 They asked, "What did she get?"

61 They answered, "A girl."

62 He said, "Have them bring it to me."

63 They brought it to him, he killed it.

64 It is the boy who remained with the captive and Kassaye.

65 For seven days.

66 His father came in the night.

67 He brought his animal and the items necessary for the naming ceremony.

68 He gave them to Kassaye.

69 He said, "Go ahead and name my son.

70 "Let them name him Mamar."

71 So they named the child in the morning.

72 Kassaye brought the necessary items, they performed the ceremony for the child, and they named him Mamar.

73 Kassaye said to name her child Mamar.

74 They called him Mamar.

75 So, the Bargantché woman nursed him all day long.

76 In the evening, Kassaye took her son.

77 She nursed him all night.

78 The Bargantché captive nursed him all day, one could see him with her.

79 When night came, Kassaye took back her son.

80 She nursed him all night.

81 It was thus, it was thus, it was thus until the child, he began to crawl.

82 When he crawls, he climbs on the feet of Si.

83 He pulls his beard.

84 Si said, "Hey! This child is suspect."

85 Kassaye said to him, "Really?

86 "He is suspect, go ahead and kill your captive's son, are you going to kill him?"

87 "If one kills the son of his captive, one will become really famous.

88 "If one kills the son of one's captive, one will become really famous, go ahead and kill."

89 "Why is he suspect? The son of your captive, do you have doubts about him too?

90 "I have given birth to eight children, you have killed all of them.

91 "The son of your captive too, you have doubts about him too.

92 "The one who killed the son of his captive, he is the one who loses.

93 Then the child walked.

94 Then the small child became a boy, a big, strong boy.

95 Then Kassaye took him by the hand to see Si, and she said,

96 "Si," and he said, "Yes?"

97 She said, "There is the son of the captive, have him care for your horse.

98 "I gave him to you so that he could be the groom for your horse.

99 "Have him go and get grass for your horse."

100 He said, "Good, may Allah be praised."

101 Si continued to have the child work.

102 Si continued to have the child work.

103 Si continued to have the child work.

104 Until, until, until, until the child became a young man.

105 He became an adolescent.

106 He became a young man tall and very strong, a tall young man.

107 The children in the compound,

108 They are the ones who insult him by saying that they don't know his father.

109 Also, they call him the little slave of Si.

110 "The little slave of Si, the little slave of Si."

111 They called him "little slave of Si," and said "We don't know your father, you don't have a father.

112 "Who is your father?"

113 Then he came home to his mother's house and told her that the children in the compound were really bothering him.

114 They say to him, "Who is your father?"

115 She told him, "Go sit down, you'll see your father."

116 He stayed there until the celebration at the end of Ramadan.

117 It is going to take place the next day.

118 Tomorrow is the celebration.
119 Soon they will look at the moon.
120 The moon will appear in a short while, and they will celebrate the next day.
121 It is in the night that the djin came to her,
122 For the man is a djin.
123 He is also a chief of the town under the river, his land that he rules.
124 It is under the river that lies the country he rules.
125 That night he called her.
126 He came, the man came to Kassaye's house.
127 He took a ring off his middle finger.
128 He said to her that when daylight comes,
129 "Give it to your son."
130 He should hold it in his hand.
131 If he gets to the edge of the river, then he should put the ring on his finger.
132 He will see his father.
133 She said, "So it will be."
134 Daylight came.
135 The sun was hot, I think, the sun was hot.
136 Then Kassaye called Mamar.
137 She said, "Mamar."
138 He said, "Yes."
139 She said, "Come."
140 He came.
141 She said to him, "Look, take this ring in your hand.
142 "But don't put it on your finger,
143 "Until you get to the river.
144 "Then you put it on your finger.
145 "At that moment, you will see your father."
146 Mamar took the ring to the river.
147 Then he put the ring on his middle finger.
148 The water opened up.
149 Under the water there are so many cities, so many cities, so many cities, so many villages, and so many people.
150 It is his father too who is the chief.
151 They too get themselves ready, they go out to go to the prayer ground.

152 He said, "That's the way it is."

153 His father greets him with an embrace.

154 There is his son, there is his son.

155 Yes, the prince whom he fathered while away,

156 The chief's son whom he fathered while away has come.

157 He said to him, "Now go return to your home, you do not stay here.

158 "Go return home."

159 His father gave him a white stallion, really white, really, really, really, really, really, really, really white like, like percale.

160 He gave him all the things necessary.

161 He gave him two lances.

162 He gave him a saber, which he wore.

163 He gave him a shield.

164 He bid him good-bye.

165 Si too and his people,

166 Si too has a daughter, two boys and one daughter that he has fathered.

167 He and his people go out, they went to the prayer ground.

168 They are at the prayer ground.

169 Then Mamar went around them and headed directly for them.

170 They were about to start the prayer.

171 They said, "Stop, just stop, a prince from another place is coming to pray with us.

172 "A prince from another place is coming to pray with us."

173 The horse gallops swiftly, swiftly, swiftly, swiftly, swiftly, swiftly he is approaching.

174 He comes into view suddenly, leaning forward on his mount.

175 Until, until, until, until, until, until, until he touches the prayer skin of his uncle, then he reins his horse there.

176 Those who know him say that he is the little captive of Si.

177 Actually, he does resemble the little captive of Si, he has the same look as the little captive of Si.

178 Did you see him! When I saw him I thought that it was the little captive of Si.

179 He retraced his path only to return again.

180 Until he brought the horse to the same place, where he reined it again.

181 Now he made it gallop again.

182 As he approaches the prayer skin of his uncle,
183 He reins his horse.
184 He unslung his lance, and pierced his uncle with it until the lance touched the prayer skin.
185 Until the spear went all the way to the prayer skin.
186 At that moment, Kassaye was among the people at the prayer ground.
187 Kassaye is in the crowd.
188 Since she knew in advance what was to happen,
189 She is among the crowd.
190 All together they reach up to grab him.
191 She said, "Let him go!
192 "Let him alone, it is Mamar, son of Kassaye.
193 "It is Mamar, the son of Kassaye, let him go.
194 "Si has killed eight of my children.
195 "You want to catch him, someone who has taken the life of one man who has himself taken eight lives—leave him alone!"
196 They let him go.
197 They took away the body, and Mamar came to sit down on the prayer skin of his uncle.
198 They prayed.
199 They took away the body to bury it.
200 That is how Mamar took the chieftaincy.
201 When they finished praying,
202 He mounted his horse, and the people followed him.
203 Then the son of his uncle says to him, "Son of Kassaye, you did it all by yourself."
204 He did it by himself *zungudaani*.
205 He did it himself, the people didn't do it.
206 Son of Kassaye, who did it himself.
207 He did it himself *zungudaani*.
208 He did it himself, the people didn't do it.
209 Kassaye glanced in back of herself to see her nephew, the son of her brother.
210 She said, "You want to shame yourself.
211 "You who are the son of the man, you want to beg for the son of the woman!"
212 He said, "Me, I sing his praises.
213 "I follow him, I become a *jeseré*, I follow him."

214 That is why we are *jeserey*.

215 He said, "Me, I am a *jeseré*, and I follow him.

216 "I put my share in his share throughout the Songhay area, and I'll take whatever I am given."

217 A griot has thus been created.

218 There's how the profession of griot begins.

219 The second son, he disappeared into the sky.

220 He brought a handful of razors, he dumped them down.

221 He became a sohanci.

222 He is at the origin of sohancis,

223 Who do circumcisions for people.

224 He became a sohanci.

225 The daughter cried out and jumped into the river.

226 She spent seven days under the water.

227 No one knew where she went.

228 It was on that day she came out as a sorko.

229 The sorkos come from her.

230 Her grandchildren are the sorkos.

231 They are not simply hunters on water, they are called sorkos.

232 It is difficult to obtain a sorko, if they tell you to look for a sorko in the countryside, now it is difficult.

233 The descendants of the daughter are called sorkos.

234 The descendants of one of the boys are called sohancis.

235 The descendants of the second son are we, the *jeserey*.

236 The descendants of the daughter are called sorkos.

237 Now, Mamar came to sit down.

238 He ruled then, he ruled, he ruled, he ruled, he converted.

239 Throughout Mamar's reign, what he did was to convert people.

240 Any village that he hears is trying to resist,

241 That is not going to submit,

242 He gets up and destroys the village.

243 If the village accepts, he makes them pray.

244 If they resist, he conquers the village, he burns the village.

245 Mamar made them convert, Mamar made them convert, Mamar made them convert.

246 Until, until, until, until, until, until he got up and said he would go to Mecca.

247 Thus he started off and went as far, as far, as far as the Red Sea.

248   He said he wants to cross.

249   They told him, "There is no path.

250   "Anyone who has killed an ancestor does not have the right to cross to Mecca.

251   "But there are two ways, three ways, so look for one you can take.

252   "Now you will return home.

253   "You must find a hen who has just produced chicks, and drive them from home.

254   "You will drive a hen who has just produced chicks and its little ones to the Red Sea.

255   "Then you can cross to go on the pilgrimage."

256   They said, "Either you go home,

257   "Or You go into the distant, uncleared bush.

258   "You clear it with your own hands.

259   "You don't let anyone help with it.

260   "You sow by your own hand without the help of anybody.

261   "You cultivate it and you recultivate it, and you leave the millet so that the birds and the wild animals may eat it.

262   "If you do that, and if you come, you can cross to go on the pilgrimage.

263   "Or you go home to start a holy war,

264   "So that you can make them submit until you reach the Red Sea.

265   "You will cross."

266   He said that he would be able to carry out the holy war.

267   Mamar went home to Gao.

268   It is at this time that he gathered together all the horses.

269   He took all the horses.

270   He began by the west.

271   You have heard that among the Mossi, there are descendants of Mamar.

272   They say that it is during this conquest that he continued to father them.

273   You have heard that they say the pure Bargantché.

274   In each ethnic group you hear about, people say there are descendants of Mamar.

275   Well, from that area where he started,

276   In each village where he stopped during the day, for example, this place,

277 If he arrives in midafternoon, he stops there and spends the night.

278 Early in the morning, they pillage and they go on to the next village, for example, Liboré.

279 The cavalier who goes there,

280 He traces on the ground for the people the plan for the mosque.

281 Once the plan for the foundation is traced,

282 The people build the mosque.

283 It is at that time,

284 Mamar Kassaye comes to dismount from his horse.

285 He makes the people—

286 They teach them verses from the Koran relating to prayer.

287 They teach them prayers from the Koran.

288 Any villages that refuse, he destroys the village, burns it, and moves on.

289 In each village where he arrives,

290 The village that he leaves in the morning,

291 The horses ride ahead.

292 They build a mosque before his arrival.

293 When he arrives, he and his people,

294 He teaches the villagers prayers from the Koran.

295 He makes them pray.

296 They—they learn how to pray.

297 After that, in the morning, he continues on.

298 Every village that follows his orders, that accepts his wishes,

299 He conquers them, he moves on.

300 Every village that refuses his demand,

301 He conquers it, he burns it, he moves on.

302 Until the day—Mamar did that until, until, until, until the day he arrived at the Red Sea.

303 It is on that day that they gave him the right to cross.

304 Before arriving at the Red Sea,

305 All the horsemen, those who died, those who were tired, returned.

306 Except for Modi Baja, Modi Baja and the *jeseré*, his cousin, who stayed with him.

307 It is they alone who remained at his side.

308 He made the crossing in their company.

309 So they arrived in Mecca.

310 He made the pilgrimage and he said then that he would like to see the tomb of Our Lord's Messenger.

311 In those days they had not built it yet.

312 He came, they told him, he said he wanted to see the tomb of Our Lord's Messenger.

313 They replied to him, "By Allah truly, the tomb, you won't see it.

314 "Because if you peek into this tomb,

315 "The thing that is in there will keep you from getting out."

316 He asked that they let him peek into it.

317 They said, "Fine, on one condition.

318 "Now have them go off to get large pieces of iron chain,

319 "To tie around his waist.

320 "Some strong men should stay behind him and hold on tightly to the chains.

321 "He too should come to the edge of the hole to peek into it."

322 He said that he would accept that.

323 They brought the iron chains, they attached them to him well.

324 The strong men stood behind and braced themselves to hold onto the chains.

325 He came to the edge of the hole.

326 He peeked into it.

327 What he found there at the bottom of that tomb,

328 It resembled young onion shoots, and it looked very soft, very soft, very soft, very soft, very soft.

329 Now, when he stood up quickly,

330 He suddenly dragged the strong men with him.

331 He then dropped into the hole, and his two arms went into the hole like that.

332 Then he grabbed and pulled, he ate, he grabbed and pulled, he ate.

333 Before they pulled him up out of the hole,

334 He grabbed and pulled out two handfuls and came out with them.

335 His cousin was standing at his right hand, he gave that to him.

336 Modi Baja was standing at his left hand, he gave that to him.

337 Modi Baja brought his from Mecca all the way home, he sold it.

338 None of Modi Baja's people suffered.

339 From that day to the present, Our Lord did not make their lives hard.

340 Our ancestor ate his.

341 He left, and he left us in suffering.

342 Since that day until the present, no descendant of Modi Baja has suffered.

343 They didn't tire from a hard life, they didn't seek to work hard in life.

344 They sup well, they lunch well, they dress well.

345 It is at that time that Mamar Kassaye retraced his steps.

346 The *jeserey* say of him,

347 "*Long live* Mamar.

348 "*Long live* Kassaye *Mamadi*.

349 Mamar son of Kassaye, he visited to Mecca.

350 He *proceeded* to Medina.

351 He prayed at Mecca, he ended the prayer in Medina.

352 He (undecipherable) *the Indigo Tree*.

353 He went three times around the Indigo Tree.

354 He repented, he repented . . . (undecipherable).

355 His sin and his *minor sin*.

356 He put them all together, and he put them all there.

357 He (undecipherable) *sword* of Dongo.

358 He slung the sword of Dongo on his shoulder.

359 It is in these terms that *jeserey* sing his praises.

360 They take it from way back all the way to there.

361 "*Long live* Mamar.

362 "*Long live* Kassaye.

363 "Your ancestor is Mamar, Mamar son of Kassaye."

364 He visited Mecca, he *proceeded* to Medina.

365 He prayed at Mecca and ended the prayer in Medina.

366 He went around the Indigo Tree (undecipherable), he went around the Indigo Tree three times, that is, the Kaaba.

367 He (undecipherable) the Indigo Tree.

368 He went around the Indigo Tree three times.

369 (undecipherable), his sin and his *minor sin*.

370 He put them all together, and he put them all there on that day.

371 He . . . (undecipherable) . . . Dongo.

372 He slung the sword of Dongo, which is truth.

373 He abandoned untruth and he took up truth on that day.

374 He went home.

375 When he arrived home, he was able to get married.

376   When he was away, when he was conquering,

377   It was then that he reached the Bargantché people.

378   When he reached those Bargantché people,

379   At the time of his departure, his mother told him, "Whatever battles you undertake,

380   "When you reach the Bargantché land,

381   "Watch out for them, because you have the milk of a Bargantché woman in your stomach.

382   "You will not be able to conquer the Bargantché.

383   "You have Bargantché milk in your stomach.

384   "Whatever cleverness you will use, if you reach the Bargantché, watch out, don't quarrel with them."

385   He went to the land of the Bargantché people,

386   He arrived among the Bargantché, he said he wants to fight them.

387   But the Bargantché defeated him.

388   They said that they would injure his horse.

389   So he withdrew, he went home to sleep.

390   Night came, late at night.

391   He got up suddenly and recited some holy words.

392   He said, among his horse, where could he find someone who could see his mother in a short time.

393   A sohanci got up quickly.

394   He said, "It is I who will see your mother."

395   He said, "What time will you come?"

396   He said, "Before the first cock crow.

397   "You will see me before daylight."

398   He said, "Good, praised be to Allah, go ahead."

399   He said, "If you leave, tell my mother:

400   "Me, I have reached the Bargantché.

401   "By Allah, I have fought against them but they have beaten me."

402   There is no longer any way of advancing.

403   The Bargantché man went out of the village.

404   He went away from the crowd, and took off all his clothes.

405   Suddenly he took off into the sky.

406   The sohanci flies fast.

407   They fly faster than airplanes.

408   They go faster than a hawk.

409   He arrived at Sikiyay, Sikiyay.

410 It is there that he arrived, he heard them say, "Sana has given birth, Sana has given birth, Sana has given birth, Sana has given birth."

411 So there he landed.

412 He hid himself as he entered into the village.

413 They said, "What are they saying?"

414 They replied; "Sana has given birth."

415 They said, "Who is Sana?"

416 They said, "Mamar Kassaye who went away, his wife whom he married before he left.

417 "Whom he left pregnant.

418 "It is that woman there who is Sana.

419 "It is that woman who gave birth to a boy in his absence.

420 "Mamar Kassaye has gone away.

421 "It is his wife who gave birth to a boy in his absence."

422 He said, "That's true."

423 He said, "Now, this son,

424 "On the day when he was old enough to be named, they gave him a name."

425 He should be given the name Daouda.

426 Daouda Sana.

427 Sana Alma Daouda.

428 Sana Boria Alma Daouda.

429 Sana Boriayze Cim Daouda.

430 He continued on his route.

431 He went to his mother's home.

432 His mother, Kassaye, had told him, "Long ago,

433 "I told him not to fight against the Bargantché.

434 "He cannot beat them, for he has in his stomach the milk of a Bargantché."

435 However, she told him,

436 Now, she took some cotton seeds in her hand and said, "Take."

437 She took an egg, a chicken egg, and she said to him, "Take."

438 She took a stone, a river stone, she told him, "Take."

439 "If you go," if he goes to the Bargantché,

440 If the Bargantché chase him,

441 He should put all his horses before him and he should be the only one behind.

442 He should scatter the cotton seeds behind him.

443 They will become a dense bushy barrier between him and them.

444 If they chop it down,

445 This dense bush will not prevent anything.

446 They will clear the bush in order to find him.

447 If the bush does not help at all,

448 This time, if they are still hunting him,

449 He should put all his cavalry in front of him.

450 He should throw the stone behind him.

451 It will become a big mountain that will be a barrier between them.

452 If the big mountain does not help them,

453 And when they chase him again,

454 He should put all his cavalry in front of him again,

455 Leaving himself in the rear.

456 He should throw the egg behind him.

457 The egg will become a river to separate them.

458 The river cannot—they will stop at the river.

459 That egg will become a river that will be a barrier between them.

460 Before the cocks crow at dawn,

461 When dawn has really come,

462 The sohanci returns, he lands on the earth.

463 He said, "By Allah, when I passed by Sikiyay I heard them say that Sana had given birth.

464 "Then I said that if Sana gives birth—since Sana had given birth,

465 "They should name the child Daouda."

466 He is the one who is Daouda Sana.

467 They continued until they . . .

468 He escaped from the Bargantché, the Bargantché who live along the river.

469 He never again fought against them.

470 Now, he just passed through their country, to go and start again his reign.

471 The day when he came back,

472 He came back to Gao.

473 The only one left with him was his *jeseré* and Modi Baja.

474 He came back.

475   He dismounted from his horse.

476   He brought together forty stallions.

477   He said that marriage should take place between him and the Songhay.

478   It is not like today during the era of the Whites.

479   Before, young Songhay men courting women didn't have anything.

480   He came back to his house.

481   So, the first child he fathered in the Songhay,

482   It is the one who is named Zara Almanyauri.

483   Zara Almanyauri the woman from the Gobir region, Zara Moussa child of the Gobir.

484   For Moussa, *what has been bound with iron can only be undone with iron.*

485   It is Moussa Zara.

486   It is she who was his first wife.

487   It is Zara who is his first wife, it is Zara who gave birth to Moussa.

488   Moussa Zara, he is the other son of Mamar.

489   After him,

490   *After him, he left,* after, he went by.

491   His name is Mahamma Damba Bana, he fathered Mohamma Gao,

492   Who *expected to ascend to the great throne of the Songhay.*

493   He is the one who expected to ascend to the great throne of the Songhay.

494   But death refused it to him, he died before his father.

495   *After he went by,* he too after him.

496   He *fathered* Jam Neera.

497   He fathered Issaka,

498   Mallam Koy Yara.

499   (undecipherable) . . . Si.

500   Issaka the good, Issaka the bad, Mallam Koy Yara.

501   (undecipherable)

502   He said that if he announces himself, the people of Mallam will hear him.

503   He said that if he doesn't announce himself, the people of Mallam will hear him.

504 What he does to them, he is going to continue to do (undecipherable).

505 In the future they will surprise him (undecipherable).

506 (undecipherable) . . . the smallest of the children,

507 Sana Alma Daouda.

508 He is called Sana Daouda.

509 Sana Boriyey.

510 Alma Daouda, Sana Boriyeze Jin Bonkani.

511 Daouda *fathered* Nyami.

512 Imama Nyami.

513 Nyami . . . Nyami . . . blacksmith . . . he ran . . . Nyami . . . pond . . .
Nyami . . . how you . . . Nyami (line partially undecipherable).

514 (undecipherable)

515 The smallest of his children, it is he who expected the throne
from his father's line.

516 (undecipherable)

517 They answered him that a little child cannot have the paternal
throne in the Songhay.

518 "(undecipherable) . . . Father, for what reason?"

519 (undecipherable)

520 (undecipherable)

521 (undecipherable)

522 The two lions who are on the road to Gombo,

523 Anyone who has not killed these lions will not have the paternal throne in the Songhay.

524 Daouda *became angry.*

525 Daouda son of Mamar got angry.

526 The horse of Daouda became angry too.

527 (undecipherable)

528 Daouda son of Mamar became angry and went to bed.

529 For seven days he didn't drink any water, any millet drink, or eat
any millet paste.

530 He went into his house, and lay down all curled up.

531 *For seven days he didn't drink any water, any millet drink, or eat any
millet paste.*

532 The horse of Daouda also became angry.

533 He too didn't drink any water, he didn't graze, didn't eat any
millet for seven days.

534 (undecipherable).

535 In the night, *late in the middle of the night,*

536 (undecipherable).

537 *At dawn a single rooster crowed and the other one replied to his call,*

538 At dawn a single rooster crowed and the other replied to his call.

539 (undecipherable).

540 He saddled his horse.

541 (undecipherable).

542 His horse paced at a slow gallop.

543 *He went off on the road to Gombo.*

544 He went off on the road to Gombo.

545 *Daouda son of Mamar sang out.*

546 He neared the place where the lions live.

547 Daouda son of Mamar sang out.

548 (undecipherable).

549 Daouda's horse also whinnied three times.

550 (undecipherable).

551 Two lions leaped out.

552 (undecipherable).

553 (undecipherable).

554 One went to the right side, the other to the left.

555 They were waiting for him.

556 Daouda son of Mamar saw the lions, nothing came to make his heart tremble.

557 Daouda's horse saw the lions.

558 Nothing made his animal heart shiver from fear.

559 His horse picked up the pace until he reached the lions.

560 He didn't . . . (undecipherable).

561 (undecipherable)

562 One of the lions got up on his left side.

563 The other got up on his right side.

564 *He pierced the first one with a single throw of his spear.*

565 *He cut off the head of the other.*

566 He pierced one with a single throw of his spear, he knocked him down.

567 And he cut off the head of the other.

568 Daouda Mamar went back home, went into his room and went to sleep.

569 Until morning.
570 He came to the place where his half brothers met to talk.
571 He said he wanted them to give him the throne of the Songhay.
572 (undecipherable)
573 (undecipherable)
574 They told Daouda son of Mamar that a child cannot have the throne of Songhay.
575 (undecipherable)
576 Daouda Mamar asked why.
577 Whatever . . . (undecipherable).
578 The two lions who are on the road to Gombo,
579 Which make one famous . . . (undecipherable),
580 He who has not killed these two lions will not have the throne of his father in Songhay.
581 Daouda son of Mamar told the people to get up and go out onto the road to Gombo.
582 It is the real men, he said, not any men, not any people, not any men, they should select the real men who should go out onto the Gombo road.
583 If they go there,
584 The one he pierced with a single thrust of a spear, they should make a prayer skin out of it, and have it spread out in the mosque.
585 And the one that he beheaded, they should make a water-skin out of it, to put water in it for the Songhay.
586 They went out to the place where the lions were, they killed the lions.
587 They made a prayer skin with this one, they came and put it in the mosque.
588 With the other, they made a water-skin for fetching water in the Songhay.
589 Daouda, son of Mamar.
590 So, Daouda, the son of Mamar.
591 He is the one who is Namaro.
592 The chief of Namaro who is there now,
593 He is Doudou.
594 Doudou was fathered by Bonwala.
595 Bonwala Mamadou.

596 Karidio Mamadou.

597 Kalilou Mamadou.

598 Mamadou Djinde Marria.

599 Hamsou Djinde Marria.

600 She is the one they took to Kannarey.

601 It is she who is the ancestor of the people of Kannarey.

602 It is Hamsou Djinde Marria whom they married and took away.

603 It is she who is the ancestor of the people of Kannarey.

604 Sidi Djinde Marria.

605 Djinde Marria Dosso Kayne.

606 Dosso Kayne Kobakire.

607 Kobakire Issaka.

608 Issaka Sorkayze.

609 Sorkeyze Beri, Daouda Sorkeyze Beri.

610 Now that the people of Namaro are the descendants of Daouda son of Mamar.

611 The people of Karma come from there too.

612 Karma too today.

613 It is Tinni who is the chief.

614 Tinni too, the son of Nouhou.

615 Nouhou too, the son of Baouna.

616 Baouna Albanna.

617 Kalfarma Albanna.

618 Gabilinga Albanna.

619 Kalmassikorey Albanna.

620 Albanna Issaka.

621 Issaka Koberika.

622 Kobay Fari Monzo.

623 Fari Monzo Walci.

624 Walci Daouda.

625 Daouda, son of Mamar.

626 In those days they would say, "*Long live* Mamar, *long live* Kassaye *Mamadi.*

627 "Your ancestor is Mamar Kassaye.

628 "He visited Mecca, he went up to Medina.

629 "He prayed at Mecca, he ended the prayer in Medina.

630 "He (undecipherable) the Indigo Tree, he went three times around the Indigo Tree.

631   "He *repented*."
632   "He *repented* . . . (undecipherable).
633   "His sin and his *minor sin*.
634   "He put them together and he put them all there.
635   "He . . . sword of Dongo . . . called . . . (partially undecipherable).
636   "He himself picked up the sword of Dongo."
637   At a single place where he *fathered* Bodronkou.
638   The first son whom he fathered in Songhay,
639   Zara Minyauri.
640   Zara Bobilantché Minyauri.
641   Zara Bobilantchéze Moussa.
642   Moussa called . . . (undecipherable).
643   Dead . . . red pepper . . . (undecipherable).
644   Moussa, son of Zara, said that he is iron.
645   Everything that is attached with iron must be undone with iron.
646   (undecipherable)
647   (undecipherable)
648   He said that he, among his rival half-brothers, is the horn of the great ram.
649   (undecipherable)
650   It is Our Lord who twisted it, nobody can straighten it out except Our Lord.
651   Moussa . . . (undecipherable).
652   (undecipherable)
653   (undecipherable)
654   He said he is iron.
655   What is attached by iron must be undone with iron.
656   Moussa . . . (undecipherable).
657   (undecipherable)
658   He said that he among his rival half brothers is the hat of a wild boar.
659   Sarey and . . . (undecipherable).
660   (undecipherable)
661   Nobody can cut if he is absent . . . (undecipherable).
662   (undecipherable)
663   (undecipherable)
664   (undecipherable)

665 (undecipherable)

666 (undecipherable)

667 He said that he among his rival half brothers is the grass at the bottom of a well.

668 The cow does not eat it, she does not fear a live coal.

669 The place where you ... (undecipherable).

670 Any cow who does eat it, she will be cut up into pieces in broad daylight.

671 Moussa ... (undecipherable).

672 (undecipherable)

673 (undecipherable)

674 He said that he among his rival half brothers is the bit and the bridle of the dove.

675 Look ... (undecipherable).

676 The blacksmith cannot make it in his absence.

677 Come ... (undecipherable).

678 Except in his presence where his eye can see it.

679 You heard ... (undecipherable).

680 It is his head that is really a big head.

681 (undecipherable) ... *departed*.

682 After Moussa, son of Zara,

683 (undecipherable)

684 He fathered Mohamma Gao.

685 Who tore off one of his testicles.

686 Who wanted to be the greatest chief of the Songhay.

687 Until (undecipherable) ... death refuses to come to him.

688 He *fathered*, fathered Salma Bala.

689 He fathered Hayssa, son of Barkounia, son of Mamar.

690 He *fathered* Jam Neera, he fathered Issaka.

691 He *fathered* Jam Neera, he fathered Issaka Mallam Koy Diara.

692 He said that when he speaks, the people of Mallam hear.

693 He said that ... (undecipherable) ... called.

694 Also, if he does not speak, the people of Mallam hear.

695 He *fathered* Sana Alma Daouda.

696 He fathered Daouda, son of Sana.

697 Sana Boriye Ma Daouda.

698 Sana Bode Jimbo Kane

699 Daouda *fathered* Nyami.

700 Imama Nyami.

701 Lamido Nyami.

702 Garesan Nyami.

703 Zuro Nyami.

704 Zuro Bongo Nyami.

705 Hamsa Alma Tchaki Nyami.

706 The grandson of Daouda Doumbo Kane.

707 Bata Sura Tchalma Daouda.

708 He fathered Daouda, son of Zatey.

709 (undecipherable) . . . Ma Daouda Farmoney.

710 The snake refuses to allow anyone to wipe his mouth.

711 Daouda, son of Zatey, refuses mockery.

712 Zide Barkatou.

713 Daouda Barmono.

714 The pebble refuses a blow on the back.

715 Daouda, son of Zatey, refuses mockery.

716 You . . . (undecipherable).

717 Daouda Barmono.

718 The hippopotamus refuses to uncover the truth.

719 Daouda, son of Zatey, refuses mockery.

720 (undecipherable)

721 Daouda Barmono.

722 The fire refuses to take it in hand.

723 Daouda, son of Zatey, refuses mockery.

724 Who . . . (undecipherable).

725 Daouda Barmono.

726 The lion refuses the saddle.

727 Daouda, son of Zatey, refuses mockery.

728 He *fathered* Wadu Karmi Badi.

729 He fathered Wadu Kayize.

730 Souleymana.

731 Hiya Mamar Kounji.

732 Mamar, Mamar Kounji.

733 He fathered Kolondia, son of Manu.

734 He *fathered* Nyao Galam Bu Di Hima.

735 He fathered Nayo Gandaize Harigoni.

736 He *fathered* Welta Selma Bazaga.

737 He fathered Watta Cissey, son of Samsou.

738 Samsou Fillo.

739 He fathered Samsou Hinka.

740 Boubey ma jimbo kaney.
741 Daouda Goubayze.
742 Jama Alma Yerima.
743 He fathered Jama, son of Baba Dosso.
744 Kormoto and Kwaley . . . (undecipherable).
745 Fabay and Badeba.
746 The village of Fabay is Deba.
747 Samo Nyamo and Bwalo.
748 The village of Sama Nyamo is Waloga.
749 The *village* of Doullo is Yeni.
750 The village of Doullo is Yeni.
751 The *village* of Zoubzoub is Kassani.
752 The village of Zoubzoub is Kassani.
753 The *village* of Ali Wuria is Bounza.
754 The village of Ali Wuria is Bounza.
755 The *village* of Alimatu comes from Soudourey.
756 The village of Alimatou is Soudourey.
757 The village of Salma . . . (undecipherable).
758 The village of Salama is Sansane-Haoussa.
759 He . . . *village* . . . (undecipherable).
760 He transformed the entire village into a . . .
      (undecipherable). . . village.
761 He . . . (undecipherable).
762 He took away their power.
763 He will . . . (undecipherable).
764 (undecipherable)
765 He did not go to group them together.
766 (undecipherable)
767 He did not reach very far.
768 He doesn't need a single one of them.
769 (undecipherable)
770 Except the sweet name of Songhay.
771 And its bad praises.
772 And its good praises.
773 He *fathered* Zourmana called Komdiago.
774 He fathered Amar, son of Zoumbani.
775 Dombika did not reach Wuriey.
776 Komdiago did not compete against them.
777 If they raced off to war,

778 The horse of Amar won.

779 The rock did not return to Wuriey.

780 Komdiago did not compete against them.

781 The master of the road refused to flee.

782 Amar's horse won.

783 The striking spirits did not reach Wuriey.

784 Komdiago didn't compete with them.

785 He raced off to war.

786 Amar's horse won.

787 It was Zoumba who was called Komdiago.

788 Amar son of Zoumba.

789 Sadjey Neri.

790 Seven mothers,

791 Mother who returned to awaken Bodronkou.

792 Which he killed himself in order to take the throne of Songhay.

793 (undecipherable)

794 (undecipherable)

795 He who did not fear for the life of his mother.

796 That person would not give a damn for the life of the mother of someone else.

797 He *fathered* Jumba called Komdiago.

798 He fathered Amar, son of Zoumba.

799 Sadjey . . . (undecipherable) . . . *King* Bodronkou.

800 He killed seven mothers himself in order to take the throne of Songhay.

801 The one who brought his Sadjey . . . (undecipherable).

802 He who did not fear for the life of his mother doesn't care about the life of someone else's mother.

803 He *fathered* Salmata.

804 Soumayla, son of Kassa.

805 Kassa and Salma Zoumou, Kassa Ouseize Soumayla.

806 He is the one they said it is true . . . (undecipherable)

807 It can be the good Soumayla Kassa.

808 It can be the bad Soumayla Kassa.

809 Zoumar came to Zokary.

810 Yorgo came . . . (undecipherable).

811 Soumayla Kassa killed Hawseizi.

812 Hawsaizina disappeared before dawn.

813 (undecipherable)

814 (undecipherable)
815 When Soumayla Kassa stops in a village,
816 It is at this moment that he proclaims himself village chief.
817 He kills a cow and entertains the village chief.
818 Soumayla Kassa, he is the one who was installed as chief of Gao.
819 He is the one who rules the country.
820 Soumayla Kassa came to take the throne.
821 It is on that day that he came to marry Sagouma.
822 Sagouma too, it is her father who died on the throne.
823 Soumayla Kassa took over the chieftaincy.
824 Soumayla Kassa took over the chieftaincy.
825 He came to sit on the throne.
826 He also has a wife whom he had married earlier.
827 This woman is of captive origin, but he did not free her.
828 She is a captive of the slave family of Sagouma,
829 Whom he married, but he did not free her.
830 He married her just like that, since he was the chief.
831 Now, he assumed the chieftaincy.
832 The father of Sagouma died,
833 The brother of Sagouma didn't inherit the throne.
834 He remained in his father's compound in a state of poverty.
835 Soumayla Kassa took the chieftaincy.
836 He married Sagouma,
837 In her father's compound, and then led her into his own compound.
838 His first wife is also a captive of the family of Sagouma.
839 When he married her he did not free her.
840 She stayed there, she stayed there, she stayed there,
841 Until, until, until he found,
842 The first wife gave birth to a single son,
843 Whom they call Amar Zoumbani.
844 It is that woman from Dabay who gave birth to him.
845 He married Sagouma.
846 Sagouma also gave birth to twins, two boys.
847 Their city of Gao knew a beautiful, rich, single woman.
848 The princes, the rich, the brave,
849 All competed for her hand.
850 Day and night the griots and molo players of Gao, the Fulani griots and molo players, the female griots,

851 All the griots are in the house of this young woman.

852 There is lots of activity all the time, handsome men and beautiful women are there.

853 For the pleasure of life.

854 Amar Zoumbani entered among the people there.

855 They say, "Now that our prince is entering the competition,

856 "We don't know what to do.

857 "We have money,

858 "Some others have money.

859 "Others have animals."

860 Others are handsome men.

861 Others are warriors.

862 "But now our prince entered the competition."

863 The prince entered into it.

864 The brother of Sagouma, who is the son of the former chief, he too enters the competition.

865 The new prince and the old prince go to see the young lady.

866 Until, until, until, until they compete with each other.

867 One day Amar Zoumbani went out by himself.

868 He said to give the Fulani griots ten horses.

869 The Fulani griots proclaim to everyone, they *stroll around*:

870 The prince gave them ten horses.

871 The prince gave them ten horses.

872 They are really happy.

873 That thing there,

874 It bothered these people.

875 It bothered the princes and the rich people.

876 They remained like that, until evening.

877 The son of the former chief,

878 Got up and went back into the compound of his father.

879 He came to sit down, very sad, his head on his legs.

880 Now his father is no longer a chief.

881 That night Sagouma, who is the sister, came out of her husband's compound, the new chief's compound.

882 She came into this compound, she found her brother sitting in his father's compound.

883 She said to him, "What is it that makes this so-and-so so sad?"

884 He said, "No, nothing is bothering me."

885 She replied, "You are lying, it is because you are not worthy men.

886 "I heard since noon, I heard what happened.

887 "They say, 'Amar Zoumbani gave the Fulani griots ten horses.'

888 "The Fulani griots are showing their joy everywhere for Amar Zoumbani.

889 "Well, since Amar Zoumbani has given ten horses to the griots,

890 "Why didn't you take the wrist of the son of your captive and offer it to the griots?

891 "It is the son of your captive.

892 "If he has given the Fulani griots ten horses, you too, you have given them a captive.

893 "The son of your captive.

894 "When he gave ten horses to the griots,

895 "You too, take him by the hand.

896 "You say it is the son of your captive.

897 "You too have given a captive to the griots."

898 Today he returned.

899 The next day, they got together again.

900 Amar Zoumbani said that he gave the Songhay griots, the Fulani griots, another ten horses.

901 The other man grabbed the hand of Amar Zoumbani who is the prince.

902 He said to the Fulani griots, "I too, I have given you a captive."

903 Now then, the crowd dispersed.

904 "The one who gave a prince in saying that he was a captive, it is you whom he gave."

905 In any case, the crowd dispersed.

906 This bothered Amar Zoumbani very, very much.

907 He came home to his father's house, he said to his father,

908 So he is a captive.

909 Soumayla Kassa said to him,

910 "You are a captive.

911 "Because, when I married your mother, I did not buy her freedom.

912 "It is the captive of someone else whom I married.

913 "It is also the captive who gave birth to you.

914 "If at least I had freed your mother—

915 "But to tell the truth, I didn't free her.

916 "Everything they tell you is true."

917 Amar Zoumbani went away to sit down.

918 The feast, the feast of Tabaski was coming.

919 The brother of Sagouma who is the son of the former chief,

920 He has one male horse that he inherited from his father.

921 It is a black stallion with no white markings anywhere.

922 No being could have such a black coat.

923 He is with his horse in the family compound.

924 If his brother-in-law who is the current chief mounts, he follows him on this particular horse.

925 When Amar Zoumbani got mad,

926 The feast was approaching.

927 He said to his father, "Tomorrow morning is the holiday.

928 "A black horse that has no white markings,

929 "It is on this that I will mount to go to the holiday.

930 "If it is not on this that I will mount, I will not go off to the prayer."

931 His father said to him, "You will go if the Lord wishes it."

932 So, Soumayla Kassa had the horsemen mount.

933 He told them to go back to the Songhay.

934 To look into all the corners of the country,

935 To see if they could find a black horse with no white markings.

936 The horsemen spent two or three days, they went everywhere in the Songhay.

937 They didn't find a stallion, they didn't find a black stallion that didn't have white marks.

938 Every black horse they heard about,

939 If they went off to look at it, it had white markings.

940 Until the night before the holiday.

941 One evening they went off into an area.

942 A dark horse with white markings.

943 That horse was dark with white markings.

944 He had some white markings.

945 They caught him and brought him to Soumayla Kassa.

946 In the middle of the night they brought him.

947 The holiday will take place in the morning, when it is light.

948 They tell him that they have covered all of the Songhay.

949 They couldn't find a black horse.

950 But they found a horse spotted with white.

951   They say that between now and morning he will be transformed into a dark horse.

952   "Get out the black clothing,

953   "To soak them in water in order to rub the horse."

954   They went to get out the black clothes, they soak them in water to wash the horse.

955   They spent the whole night rubbing the horse, before dawn the horse was completely black.

956   All the white hair was black because of the indigo.

957   In the morning he said to his son, "Here is the horse."

958   The son said that what he saw was good, now his heart was refreshed.

959   He will go to the prayer ground.

960   They prepared to go to the prayer ground.

961   He said,

962   To go call for him his brother-in-law.

963   They went off to call his brother-in-law.

964   They said, "Soumayla Kassa is calling you."

965   He came to say to his brother-in-law,

966   "Now, you see, I cannot go to the prayer.

967   "There is an affair that prevents me from going.

968   "So you too must not go.

969   "The thing that prevents me from going there warrants that we should stay together.

970   "So, I am not going to the prayer, you too must not go.

971   "The thing that prevents me from going there warrants that we should stay together.

972   "Before people leave the prayer, we are going to do what we are planning to do."

973   He knows that if his brother-in-law goes to the prayer on his horse.

974   His son will see the horse.

975   And it is at the prayer that they will throw spears at each other.

976   Because his son wants only the horse of his brother-in-law.

977   "May they take away his horse in order to give it to him."

978   It is the horse of the brother-in-law of Soumayla Kassa that he is looking for.

979   But the brother-in-law did not go to the prayer.

980 Amar Zoumbani directs the people.
981 They go off to the prayer ground.
982 They are returning.
983 The one who got, I think, father, the horse of a competing brother, the one who got the horse of a competing brother,
984 Spurs and then reins his horse.
985 Spurs and then reins his horse.
986 Spurs and then reins his horse.
987 His *jeseré* is with him.
988 Until, until, until, until the moment when they are almost at their house.
989 The horse is covered with sweat.
990 Sweat, if it wets indigo, it causes the indigo to run.
991 The horse is sweating.
992 The sweat now causes the indigo to run, all the sweat on all of the body, wherever it is wet all over, it causes the indigo to bleed.
993 The sweat causes the indigo to run.
994 The white clothes that they were wearing are all dirty because of the sweat of the horse.
995 The *jeseré* who accompanies him, who accompanies him, flatters him.
996 The *jeseré* changes language and speaks Soninké, he says, "Although they say that this is a black horse, it is a white horse."
997 It is these words that fell into his ear.
998 He said, "Although they say that this is a black horse, it is a white horse."
999 He too heard the Soninké words of the *jeseré*.
1000 He glanced behind.
1001 All his clothes were ruined by the indigo that had dyed the horse.
1002 Then, zip, he jumped.
1003 He jumped down, threw his shield on the ground suddenly, he jumped down.
1004 He unsheathed his sword and he cut the tendons of two legs of the animal.
1005 He came to sit down on his shield.
1006 He placed his sword on his feet.

1007 The horse was thrashing out of control.

1008 They went to tell his father.

1009 They said to the father, "Amar Zoumbani has killed the horse."

1010 He told them to bring the horse.

1011 Before their return, the brother-in-law returned home.

1012 They went to get it, they brought the horse back.

1013 They remained there, they remained there.

1014 Then he began to cry, Amar Zoumbani began to cry,

1015 Then he began to cry, then he began to cry.

1016 By the time the sun reached noon, say when it turns toward early afternoon,

1017 The Father was taken by his tears.

1018 Soumayla Kassa got angry.

1019 So he said to the captives,

1020 He asked them to go behind the house.

1021 The ram and everything else for the Tabaski holiday were in the compound.

1022 He told them to go behind the house,

1023 To dig a hole for him.

1024 They dug a wide, deep hole.

1025 He told them to place millet stalks over the hole.

1026 They placed millet stalks over the hole.

1027 He told them to put a grass mat on top of the stalks.

1028 They put the mat on it.

1029 He told them to spread some sand on it.

1030 He stopped on the other side of the hole.

1031 He ordered them to go tell his brother-in-law that he was calling him.

1032 They went off to call the brother-in-law.

1033 They told him that the chief was calling him.

1034 He came into the compound, he announced his arrival.

1035 They told him he was behind the house.

1036 He said, "Come to find him behind the house so that you can speak to him."

1037 Some stalks of millet, a grass mat, and some sand, can they support a person?

1038 He stepped onto the mat, then, whoops, he fell into the hole.

1039 He cried out to the captives, telling them to dump the dirt on him.

1040   They poured the dirt on him, they tamped it down.

1041   Her captive artisan that her father had left her as a legacy, a female leatherworker,

1042   She too had come to offer holiday wishes to Sagouma.

1043   Sagouma was lying on her bed.

1044   She is wishing a happy holiday to her.

1045   It is the captive who enters into the room,

1046   To open the window.

1047   She sees everything that happens.

1048   The way in which they made him fall into the hole and how they dumped the earth on him.

1049   The artisan came back to stop next to Sagouma.

1050   She says to Sagouma, "I'm going to explode, I'm going to explode."

1051   She says, "No, don't explode, wait until you arrive at your prince's house."

1052   She says, "Sagouma, I am going to explode, Sagouma, I am going to explode."

1053   She says, "No, don't explode, leave it until you arrive at your prince's house."

1054   She says, "Sagouma, I am going to explode, Sagouma, I am going to explode."

1055   She says, "No, don't explode, leave it until you arrive at your prince's house."

1056   She said, "Sagouma, I'm going to explode, Sagouma, I'm going to explode."

1057   She tells her, "Yes, yes, yes, little griotte, explode.

1058   "Tell me what you saw."

1059   The artisan tells her, "I have seen in truth,

1060   "The eye sees the misfortune."

1061   She says, "Soumayla Kassa has killed my prince."

1062   She says, "What?"

1063   She replies, "In truth, he has killed him."

1064   Sagouma replies, "That's it."

1065   Sagouma called her little slave.

1066   Sagouma also is a woman who plays the godji,

1067   For singing to princes.

1068   She called her little slave, she came.

1069   She told her to take her basket.

1070   She took her basket, she placed it outside.

1071   She told her to take her godji and hook it onto the basket.

1072   She took the godji and hooked it to the basket.

1073   She put on her clothes, and covered her head with a piece of cloth.

1074   She told her captive to take the basket.

1075   The captive took the basket.

1076   Sagouma turned around to leave.

1077   Her twin sons,

1078   They cried to come grab hold of their mother.

1079   Then she took one by his two ankles and smashed him against the wall.

1080   This one died; she threw him out.

1081   She then grabbed the other by the ankles and picked him up.

1082   He too she smashed against the other side of the wall.

1083   This one too was killed; she threw it out.

1084   She said to the captive, "Let's go."

1085   The captive followed her.

1086   This is how Sagouma went wandering in the bush.

1087   She left Gao.

1088   For seven years Sagouma was in the country of the Arma.

1089   Every Arma who called himself brave,

1090   If she hears your name, she comes to you.

1091   She would say, "So and so, I have come to visit you."

1092   He would say, "Welcome, Sagouma."

1093   "I came so that you could marry me.

1094   "Do you love me or do you not love me?"

1095   He says, "Frankly, I love you, Sagouma.

1096   "A man does not flee you, Sagouma.

1097   "That's really true."

1098   "Good, if you wish, you can marry me.

1099   "My dowry is Soumayla Kassa.

1100   "The bull sacrificed at the marriage will be Amar Zoumbani.

1101   "Any man who has not killed these two men will not marry me."

1102   Before she finishes her words, a drop of sweat falls from the head of the man onto his toe.

1103   He says to her, "Sagouma, in all candor, I can't do it."

1104   No man wants to fight with Soumayla Kassa.

1105   No man, no man would want to challenge Soumayla Kassa.

1106   He says to her, "Sagouma, in all candor, I can't do it."

1107   She says, "Fine," and passes by you.

1108   She walks on so long, walks on so long, walks on so long, for so many years in the country of the Arma.

1109   Then she heard again about an Arma who is more courageous than the other.

1110   She goes off again down there.

1111   She goes, she comes, and she tells him,

1112   "I came to visit you."

1113   He told her, "Welcome, Sagouma."

1114   "I came so that you could marry me.

1115   "Do you love me or do you not love me?"

1116   He replies, "Sagouma, a man does not flee Sagouma.

1117   "I really love you, in truth, I love you."

1118   "Good, since you love me,

1119   "My dowry is Soumayla Kassa.

1120   "The bull sacrificed at the marriage is Amar Zoumbani.

1121   "Any man who has not killed these two men,

1122   "Before me, then, the man will not marry me."

1123   He tells her, "Truly, I can't do it."

1124   "You can't do it?"

1125   He says that he really can't do it.

1126   She moves on.

1127   Until, until, until, until, until, until she arrives at the house of an Arma,

1128   Who is called Bayero.

1129   She arrives at Bayero's house.

1130   She says to Bayero, "I have come."

1131   Bayero says to her, "Welcome, Sagouma."

1132   She tells him, "I came so that you could marry me."

1133   He says, "I really love you, I, myself, and am pleased too."

1134   "Since you want to marry me,

1135   "The dowry is Soumayla Kasa.

1136   "The bull sacrificed at the marriage will be Amar Zoumbani.

1137   "Any man who has not killed these two men,

1138   "Will not, will not become married to me."

1139 He says, "Me, I have heard, that has pleased me, and I can do it."
1140 She says, "You can?"
1141 He says, "I can."
1142 She says to him, "You can?"
1143 He says to her, "I can."
1144 She says to him, "Here I have been wandering in the bush for seven years, in the country of the Arma; I have not found a man who says he can do it."
1145 He says, "I can do it, and I am going to leave."
1146 She says, "Good, praise be to Allah."
1147 "Good, I too have heard—
1148 He says, "It has been seven years that you've been in the bush.
1149 "Me too, I want you to wait for me for seven months while I get ready."
1150 She says, "Me too, I grant it to you."
1151 He too, all of his land from end to end,
1152 In all the kingdom of Badal,
1153 Bayero, Kilinsi, Zamgam, Foronkondi, they are the Arma who voted for him, they are four.
1154 All have voted for Bayero.
1155 They say they are in the war up to their necks.
1156 He says good, now inform the rich people of the country,
1157 That he will attack Gao.
1158 That he is waiting for the voices of the rich, that he is waiting for their contribution.
1159 The rich say that they have heard, but to wait a bit so that they can discuss it among themselves.
1160 He says that they should inform the chiefs, all the chiefs of the land,
1161 That he is going to attack Gao.
1162 That they should say what they are going to bring to him as aid.
1163 The chiefs said that they have heard, but to wait a bit so that they can discuss it among themselves.
1164 Like the government people who meet, these people too will meet.
1165 He said to inform the marabouts,
1166 That they were going to attack Gao.
1167 The marabouts should say what their contribution will be.

1168 The marabouts too said to wait while they discuss it among themselves.

1169 The chiefs met, and they said "What kind of aid are we going to give Bayero,

1170 "Who is about to go to war against Gao?"

1171 The chiefs swore, they voted.

1172 They said, "Good, each day that awakens,

1173 "Each sun that rises,"

1174 All the chiefs agreed.

1175 Each sun that rises,

1176 One hundred horses are on their way to supply them.

1177 Every morning one hundred horsemen mount their horses.

1178 Every morning one hundred horsemen mount their horses.

1179 Every morning one hundred horsemen mount their horses.

1180 Until the day that they conquer Gao.

1181 Until the day when they will return.

1182 Every morning one hundred horsemen mount their horses.

1183 He said he was waiting for help from the village chiefs.

1184 The rich people said good, now they too had heard.

1185 They too, each morning would appear sorghum, millet, milk, butter, rice, and dried millet paste.

1186 Every morning one hundred dugout canoes follow him.

1187 They too, the rich people, there is their contribution.

1188 Every morning one hundred dugout canoes would follow him.

1189 Butter, millet, rice, milk, sorghum, and dried millet paste.

1190 What the horses eat and what they themselves eat.

1191 Every morning one hundred dugout canoes follow him.

1192 The rich people take on that responsibility.

1193 The marabouts of the country have said that they too, every morning they will say the prayer of supplication for him.

1194 It is on that day that he mounted and went out.

1195 He went out with the horses who amounted to ten thousand who followed him.

1196 Every morning one hundred horses follow him.

1197 The first night one hundred horses followed him.

1198 The second night one hundred horses left early in the morning.

1199 The third night one hundred horses left early in the morning.

1200   All day long.
1201   Every morning one hundred horses leave early.
1202   Every morning one hundred dugout canoes with food are leaving early to follow him.
1203   In this war, the women are involved.
1204   Many, many women are in the war.
1205   They are the ones who make the food for the crowd; they are eating.
1206   They don't go to someone's house looking for food.
1207   They don't go to someone's house looking for water.
1208   The women who are in the war, they are the ones who make the food for the war; they are eating.
1209   The millet that the horses eat, it is they who bring it every morning.
1210   The sorghum that the horses eat, they bring it every morning.
1211   The milk they drink, the butter they eat,
1212   Everything together, they bring it every morning.
1213   Until the day when they arrive at Gao.
1214   They spent seven months.
1215   Each morning they attack the city of Gao.
1216   The city remains intact, it didn't even know anything was happening.
1217   Each morning they attacked all parts of the city.
1218   The city remains intact, it didn't even know anything was happening.
1219   If they have spent the morning warring, when the city counter-attacked,
1220   Before the sun sets,
1221   It has killed more than ten thousand of their horses.
1222   The next day ten thousand horses reappear.
1223   They sleep.
1224   Tomorrow they get up early in the same way and again go back to the same thing.
1225   When the people attack again, they kill more than ten thousand horses.
1226   They return to the place where they were before.
1227   Nothing diminishes in the city.
1228   At Gao, nothing diminishes.
1229   Sagouma and her lover are seated there.

1230   The war is raging, and they are seated there.

1231   Until, until, until, until it reached . . .

1232   The tooru who watch out for the city of Gao.

1233   There is a python at the edge of the river.

1234   This python never moves.

1235   He does not eat, he doesn't go out to eat in the bush, he doesn't get up.

1236   He is a tooru, all rolled up at the edge of the river.

1237   A laying hen is at the edge of the river.

1238   A black hen is on her eggs.

1239   She doesn't lay eggs, she doesn't get up, she doesn't go out into the bush.

1240   It is a tooru, it is always down there, it is down there.

1241   There is a black ox on the island.

1242   He is standing up, he looks at the east all the time.

1243   He doesn't eat, he doesn't go out into the bush, he doesn't move around.

1244   Each night he is there, looking to the east, he is there all the time.

1245   It is a tooru.

1246   In Gao, it is to these toorey that they appeal.

1247   It is with those things there that they have protected the city of Gao from all surprises.

1248   They tell them in any case that the day when a war will destroy Gao,

1249   The ox who is on the island, he will go into the water.

1250   Where he goes, if he goes into the river, where he goes,

1251   The country will move toward that spot.

1252   The python too will follow his path.

1253   It will follow the ox.

1254   The laying hen also will get up on that day and will go into the river.

1255   She will follow the path of that ox.

1256   But, in any case, if they follow different paths,

1257   The country will be destroyed.

1258   But if they follow their path, it will be saved.

1259   Thus they stayed there and the war continued . . . (undecipherable).

1260   Now the Arma are getting used to the city.

1261   When war is over for the day, they visit each other.

1262   They chat and play dili.

1263   They do everything, and in the evening, they come into town, they spend the whole night.

1264   The girls and young men come into town and spend the evening chatting.

1265   If there is an army, there is a battle, if the army dismounts, they stop fighting among themselves.

1266   One night,

1267   They are falling asleep, they are—

1268   They are chatting.

1269   A young Arma is courting an older, unmarried woman.

1270   The "girl" said to him,

1271   When the conversation was quite lively,

1272   The "girl" said to him, "Ah, our city of Gao, you cannot destroy it."

1273   He said to her, "Why?"

1274   She answered, "There is why you will not destroy our city of Gao.

1275   "At the first cock crow,

1276   "The entire city goes up in the air.

1277   "Everything you do, with your guns, it is on the ground that you shoot.

1278   "The city moves up above,

1279   "Until noon, when the horses come down.

1280   "It is at that time that the city comes back to its original place."

1281   Before the father of the "girl" could cry out at her,

1282   The "girl" had told the secret of the destruction of the city.

1283   When daylight came,

1284   The Arma mount their horses.

1285   The Arma man who had the secret,

1286   He said, "Now,

1287   "Strike, fire first into the air while waiting.

1288   "Let's shoot to see."

1289   They fired a volley.

1290   "If that doesn't work, let's shoot in the sky, let's see."

1291   So, they fired their guns into the air.

1292   One sees nothing but smoke and dust.

1293   Well, it is on this day that Sagouma became angry.

1294   When they destroyed Gao, her heart trembled; on that day she thought about the compound of her mother.

1295   It is on that day that she thought of the compound of her father,

1296   Of how the war destroyed Gao.

1297   The compound of her mother is there, the compound of her father is there.

1298   Her entire family lives in Gao.

1299   And she went to get a war to destroy Gao.

1300   It is on this day that she became heartsick.

1301   (undecipherable)

1302   They went, they destroyed Gao.

1303   The ox went downriver.

1304   The python went downriver.

1305   The laying chicken went downriver.

1306   The entire town of Gao went downstream.

1307   The dugout canoes of Gao,

1308   The dugout canoes of the Arma,

1309   The horse of Gao,

1310   The horse of the Arma,

1311   The horse are on the shore, they attack each other, they go downriver.

1312   The dugout canoes are in the water, the boatmen are stabbing each other, they are going downstream.

1313   The war continues, they are going downriver.

1314   The war rages on, they are going downriver.

1315   The horses are killing each other on the shore.

1316   The boatmen are in the water, they are killing each other.

1317   Until, until, until, until, until

1318   The moment when they arrived in the Songhay country.

1319   Sagouma and her Arma are sitting in one of the dugout canoes off to one side.

1320   It is there that life begins to please the Arma man.

1321   He says to Sagouma, "Although they say that Soumayla Kassa is a great warrior,

1322   "From the beginning of our war until the present, we haven't seen each other."

1323   She says to him, "Hey!

1324   "Stay in your place.

1325   "That man is not the kind of man that a man expects to have
      going against him face to face."

1326   He says to her, "If you know how I can go about seeing him,
      let me know."

1327   She says to her captive, "Give me the godji."

1328   The captive took the godji out of the basket, she gave it to her.

1329   She rubbed the rosin on the godji until it was ready.

1330   She tuned the godji.

1331   Then she put the godji on her feet.

1332   The Arma man is sitting.

1333   Sagouma is sitting, she places the godji on her feet.

1334   Sagouma played the godji.

1335   It is on this day that she says:

1336   Kasa Almadu Nye.

1337   Kasa Almadu Nye.

1338   Kasa wa Salma Gume.

1339   Kasa wa Seyze Soumayla.

1340   Cimingiri wa Zuma Kwayne.

1341   Nimingiri wa Zuma Kwayne.

1342   Evil one Soumayla Kassa.

1343   The evil person too, Soumayla Kassa.

1344   (undecipherable)

1345   (undecipherable)

1346   Soumayla Kassa too, eats . . . (undecipherable).

1347   Early in the morning, one can't find him there.

1348   (undecipherable)

1349   (undecipherable)

1350   (undecipherable)

1351   (undecipherable)

1352   If Soumayla Kassa stops at a village,

1353   He makes himself chief.

1354   He kills a cow and makes himself village chief.

1355   She continues to praise her husband.

1356   She continues to praise her husband.

1357   She continues to praise her husband.

1358   Soumayla Kassa is standing on a dune.

1359   He hears the godji.

1360   Then he took his stallion and drove it hard into the river.

1361   Until, until, until, until, until he arrived at the dugout canoe.

1362   Then he grabbed his lance.

1363   Before the Arma man had a chance to get ready.

1364   He pierced him with one thrust of the lance.

1365   He picked him up, he took him out of the dugout canoe.

1366   He threw him in the river.

1367   She said to him, "I already told you so.

1368   "I said that you must not wish to engage the other.

1369   "He is not a man you can meet in competition."

1370   Now the war of the Arma ended in failure.

1371   They are in the process of deploying their forces.

1372   The Songhay and they are choking each other, they are chok-
       ing each other.

1373   Until, until, until, until the moment when,

1374   They reached the right bank of the Songhay.

1375   The dugout canoes are in the water, the horses have mounted
       on the right shore.

1376   On the right bank is where the horses became thirsty.

1377   The horses are thirsty and the cavaliers are thirsty.

1378   The horses are thirsty and the cavaliers are thirsty.

1379   To the point, to the point, to the point that they don't know
       what to do.

1380   They went away from the river.

1381   A village that heard that war was coming,

1382   The people fled into their fields in the bush.

1383   Just as if it were yesterday.

1384   They went to pound millet for donu and then follow the war.

1385   They put into a clay pot the liquid left over after washing the
       millet.

1386   They put the pot down,

1387   To go down to the river.

1388   They spent the day pounding millet, they prepared their millet
       and milk porridge, and in the evening they left.

1389   It was the next day at noon that the war came to this spot.

1390   Amar Zoumbani saw the pot next to a kokorbey tree.

1391   Zip! he jumped down from his horse.

1392   Then he plunged his mouth into the clay pot.

1393   He drank, he drank, he drank, he drank until he had quenched
       his thirst.

1394   He remounted his horse,

1395 To go look for his father.
1396 He said to his father, "Come, Father, I saw some water."
1397 He replied, "Praise be to Allah."
1398 Then his father followed him with his stallion.
1399 Until they arrived at the clay pot.
1400 He said, "There is the water."
1401 Then Soumayla Kassa peeked into the clay pot.
1402 He said, "That's the water?"
1403 He said, "That's the water."
1404 He said, "You drank some?"
1405 He said, "By Allah, I did drink some."
1406 He said, "Did you quench your thirst?"
1407 He said, "I quenched my thirst."
1408 He said, "Is it that water there that you wanted me to come drink?"
1409 He said, "I saw that you were thirsty, it was for that reason that I asked you to come to drink the water."
1410 He said, "What misfortune!
1411 "Even if one buys a house cat for 50,000 francs, it will only catch mice.
1412 "You have returned home, Amar Zoumbani, you have returned home, you have returned home.
1413 "I didn't want this from you."
1414 What does this mean, he has returned home?
1415 The fact of being a captive, that is the insult that he made to him.
1416 He said, "Even if one buys a house cat for 50,000 francs, it will only catch mice."
1417 He insulted him as a captive.
1418 The fact of drinking his own mother's breast milk,
1419 That is the insult which he gave to him.
1420 This hurt Armar Zoumbani.
1421 His father put his spear in, he stirred the contents of the clay pot.
1422 He said to him, "Look, you drank water fouled with millet."
1423 "If you are not a captive, you do not come to drink water fouled with millet and say that it is ordinary water."
1424 Well, on that day, during the night, in the village where they were going to spend the night,

1425 They too, the secret that they made in their village in order to protect themselves against misfortune,

1426 Is that now,

1427 According to the seer, however noble a fast horse may be,

1428 One must not get off a horse and mount again in the morning.

1429 After that, wherever they spent the night,

1430 All his horse should be careful about going into town.

1431 For if a single man goes into town to get into trouble,

1432 Tomorrow will be the end of the war for them.

1433 The village in which the cavaliers will spend the night,

1434 That evening,

1435 Amar Zoumbani who is his son,

1436 He said to look for him wherever is found a beautiful woman, and to bring her to him.

1437 They will sleep together today.

1438 In the morning, he gets off the horse, he asks the cavaliers to bring him another horse.

1439 The crowd calls out, "Amar Zoumbani, you have ruined our war.

1440 "You thought that the dismounting ruined the war."

1441 He said they should take the saddle off the other horse and put it on his horse.

1442 They saddled the horse for him.

1443 Toward the middle of the day,

1444 The Armas came in their dugout canoes.

1445 Everything from the Songhay people, everything from the Arma,

1446 Those that they killed are dead, the ones they did not kill retreated.

1447 Amar Zoumbani has destroyed the war.

1448 The Arma pass.

1449 All the cavaliers, the Songhay people . . . took all the horses of the Arma . . . (undecipherable).

1450 The horses of the Arma did not return home.

1451 The horses, every one of them, perished.

1452 Wherever they go, the Songhay gather them up and kill them.

1453 All the Arma horses did not return.

1454 All the horses . . . (undecipherable).

1455 The dugout canoes are crossing.

1456 They are going downriver, I don't know where Our Lord may stop them.

1457 Well, it is for that reason that Mali awoke.

1458 Mali heard—dugout canoes—the Arma war that Soumayla Kassa started.

1459 It is on that day that Mali got up—at Sargan.

1460 He went off to the war against the Arma.

1461 He came to help Soumayla Kassa.

1462 He too, when he consulted about the war,

1463 The consultation that they conducted among themselves,

1464 They consulted and they consulted again.

1465 They said that the son of their sister, who is Yefarma Issaka,

1466 If Yefarma Issaka goes off to participate in this war, he will be the first to die.

1467 They consulted, and they consulted again.

1468 If Yefarma Issaka goes off to participate in this war, he will be the first to die.

1469 Any war involving Mali too,

1470 If Yefarma Issaka is not part of the war, then he won't feel happy about it,

1471 Because Yefarma is his great warrior.

1472 He is his nephew and he also is his great warrior.

1473 This seer leaves, another one comes in.

1474 He says to go look for yet another one.

1475 That one arrives, he consults, he says,

1476 "By Allah, if Yefarma goes off to war, he will be the first to die."

1477 Mali reflects on how he is going to go about,

1478 Keeping Yefarma from going.

1479 So, in the morning,

1480 On the day the war is getting ready to start,

1481 Yefarma doesn't know what is happening.

1482 He says to Yefarma that he should come—on his horse—there is an affair that needs to be handled in Foga.

1483 The chief of Foga.

1484 Among all of his horses, he doesn't see a single one in the area capable of going to Foga, except for Yefarma.

1485 He said to Yefarma he should come, he is going to send him to the chief of Foga.

1486 He spoke to him, he bid him good-bye.

1487 Yefarma left.

1488 Mali launched the war in his absence.

1489 Now they are approaching carefully, approaching carefully, approaching carefully, approaching carefully,

1490 Until the day when they dismounted at Horey Gangani.

1491 It is at the center of Horey Gangani that Mali Bero dismounted.

1492 The Arma are behind, they haven't come yet.

1493 They are waiting for the Arma.

1494 Yefarma Issaka too has left.

1495 He travels, he travels, he too.

1496 Until he goes through the Boboye, and he gets near the Zijo region.

1497 He came to the edge of a well, and he found an old captive woman who was drawing water from the well.

1498 A shallow well typical of the Boboye region.

1499 Then he said to the captive woman there, "Give me some water, I want to offer some to my horse."

1500 She replied, "By Allah, I won't do it."

1501 He said, "You won't do it?"

1502 She replied, "By Allah, I won't do it."

1503 Zip! Yefarma dismounted.

1504 He took the bit out of the horse's mouth.

1505 He grabbed the calabash from the hand of the captive woman.

1506 He turned the clay pot.

1507 He poured water for the horse, the horse quenched his thirst.

1508 Then he put the bit back in the horse's mouth.

1509 The captive woman cried and rubbed her eyes.

1510 She said, "It is I who am your equal.

1511 "While your uncle goes off to war with the Arma,

1512 "They said that if you go off to this war, you will die.

1513 "That is why they saved you by hiding you.

1514 "It is not a mission they sent you on.

1515 "Your uncle made you flee into hiding,

1516 "So that you wouldn't go.

1517 "They said that if you go off to the Arma war, you will die.

1518   "Your uncle is going off to the Arma war."

1519   Then he took off his zeela koy,

1520   At that time, there was a distinctive cloth called "zeela koy."

1521   He took the zeela koy from his saddle.

1522   He said to the captive woman, "Take your reward.

1523   "I haven't heard these words if it is not from your mouth."

1524   He remounted his horse.

1525   Late that evening,

1526   Just before dawn, not quite dawn,

1527   When the horse had reared after being spurred . . . (undecipherable).

1528   His horse sensed the odor of horses.

1529   It is at this moment that the horse of Yefarma neighed.

1530   The horse of Mali was grazing, he heard the whinnying.

1531   He too raised his head, he neighed, he answered him.

1532   A Fulani seer is next to Mali.

1533   Mali said, "*How awful,*" he said "O misfortune, here comes Yefarma."

1534   Then the Fulani laughed.

1535   He said to the Fulani, "Why are you laughing?"

1536   He told him, "Say what you've seen concerning the horses."

1537   He said, "No, never."

1538   He said, "You must tell.

1539   "Whatever you will say, I already have news of it."

1540   He said, "The horse that neighed told me that from wherever he has left and to wherever he is going, and to wherever he is coming, he and his owner have not found any brave warriors sleeping in those places.

1541   "Yours, who responded, told me that whatever the value of you and your owner,

1542   "By tomorrow morning your owner will be struck by iron."

1543   He said to him, "I know about that."

1544   Yefarma came to dismount.

1545   He began to scold his uncle.

1546   He began to scold his uncle.

1547   He began to scold his uncle.

1548   "It is I who finish this particular war.

1549   "Such-and-such a war, it is I who will win it, such-and-such a war I will win.

1550 "You are my uncle, you are my father, you are my commander-in-chief.

1551 "It is your reputation that will be made.

1552 "It is I who will win the war, for your reputation.

1553 "Warrior so-and-so, it is I who killed him, warrior so-and-so, it is I who killed him.

1554 "It is your reputation that is being made.

1555 "A man who has destroyed a good number of war drums.

1556 "You have killed many warriors.

1557 "From which war are you going to make me flee?

1558 "Why do you make me run from death?

1559 "As long as there are people, you know that a man will kill you."

1560 He said to him, "You too," he hung his head.

1561 In the morning the Arma begin to come.

1562 To the edge of Torsho.

1563 They drive the horses into the water,

1564 In order to capture a loaded dugout canoe.

1565 They make people lie down and they kill them.

1566 They drive their horses into the water again, they catch another dugout canoe load of Arma.

1567 They make them lie down, they kill them.

1568 Before the sun rises the rays are beginning to shine.

1569 They say that the horses came near the Armas' dugout canoes.

1570 An Arma is crouching next to a dugout canoe with a poisoned arrow.

1571 Then he shoots him in the middle of the heart.

1572 Yefarma brings the dugout canoe to the river's edge.

1573 They killed the Arma.

1574 They pulled the iron out, they removed it.

1575 They heated butter to put on the place.

1576 The Arma were not able to move forward.

1577 It is there too that their dugout canoes had to retreat.

1578 Mali pursued them.

1579 He pursued them, he pursued them, he pursued them, he pursued them.

1580 Until he arrived at Mayma Darou Koba.

1581 The dune of Boubon which is next to the river.

1582 It is there that he came to the shade of a koba tree.

1583 He took his spear.

1584 He said, "Who will cross?"

1585 Mali's horse stopped there.

1586 It is there that Yefarma died.

1587 When he was about to die,

1588 He asked that they look where the arrow had hit him.

1589 All *lucky* meat that is there,

1590 Wherever *lucky* meat is found,

1591 They should remove that part to give to his descendants.

1592 That is why the Gollé, wherever there is *lucky* meat,

1593 They ask for brisket.

1594 That is why the Gollé always take the brisket.

1595 If a person is not from the Gollé people, and if he takes some brisket, he lies.

1596 But today times have changed, there is lots of meat.

1597 Good meat, everybody will say, it is your share.

1598 All those who are not descended from Yefarma will not eat brisket.

1599 It is there that they buried Yefarma.

1600 The descendants settled in Boubon forever.

1601 Afterward they migrated, then they returned to Boubon.

1602 It is those people, the Gollé of Boubon, some went to the Kourfeye region, others scattered elsewhere.

Annotations

1   Nouhou Malio speaks here to the small audience assembled for his performance—some neighbors and relatives—and in particular to the researcher, who had requested that he recount the story of Askia Mohammed, known as Mamar Kassaye.

4   Si is Sonni Ali Ber.

5   The emphasis by the narrator on the common mother and father for Sonni Ali Ber and Kassaye emphasizes what should normally be a close relationship between brother and sister.

10   The interjection *Maa*—"listen" ("The seers have said 'Listen'— they told Si . . .) suggests at first a hesitation on the part of the griot between two forms of discourse. But the line also demonstrates an economical way of rendering the event's immediacy while maintaining the narrative's rapid pace.

19   There are no references anywhere in the text to the husband of Kassaye other than to the spirit who lives under the river.

43   The Bargantché live along the Niger River in a 70,000-square-kilometer area known as the Borgou in northern Benin and northwestern Nigeria. In 1968 Emmanuel Karl recorded a brief account of the conflict between the Songhay and the people of the Nikki Kingdom in that area. His source, a chief griot named Boukari Bio, reported that the Songhay infiltrated into the region and refused to leave. A young warrior named Sunon Tamu was named to lead the war against them. After early defeats, they finally drove the Songhay back across the Niger River (1974, 46–50).

57   I have translated *Irkoy* as "Our Lord," a term that means literally "our ruler" and refers figuratively to Allah.

The "they" in this line refers to the people in Sonni Ali Ber's .ourage.

67   "Animal" refers to the sheep sacrificed at a naming ceremony.

118   "Celebration," from the term *mehaw*, refers to the prayers and feast at the end of Ramadan. The literal meaning of *mehaw*, however, is "to tie up the mouth" or "to fast" (Olivier de Sardan 1982, 296).

152   It is not entirely clear here who is speaking, the father or the son, but from the context it appears to be the son, Askia Mohammed.

204, 207   The meaning of the term *zungudaani* is unclear.

210–13   The description of how a griot is created here is only one of many different ones found throughout the Sahel. What is different here is that the character in question, Sonni Ali Ber's son, assumes the role of griot. He may not be of griot origin, but he becomes a griot by his actions of following and praising Askia Mohammed.

On line 212, the phrase "I sing his praises," comes as a surprise to Kassaye because of the two connotations attached to it. The verb *nwaarey* means both "to sing praises" and, by extension, "to receive rewards" for that activity. But today it has taken on the more negative connotation of begging.

Nouhou Malio does not suggest here that he or other griots are descended from this particular noble-become-griot. But a few lines later (1. 235) he does, in fact, state that Songhay griots trace their roots to this son of Sonni Ali Ber. The notion of a griot coming from the aristocracy seems to run counter to the traditionally accepted view that griots are of lower social status. But both Vincent Monteil (1968, 785–86) and Ousmane Tandina (interviews with the author, fall 1987) confirm that nobles do on occasion carry out the functions of griots either to demonstrate fealty or to earn rewards.

219–24   The description of the *sohanci* accords with the modern Songhay view that these sorcerers come from the descendants of Sonni Ali Ber. Olivier de Sardan notes that after the end of the Sonni dynasty, the *sohanci* dispersed, settling in Wanzerbé in the northwestern corner of Niger; in Boubon and Karma on the left bank of the Niger, not far upstream from Niamey; in Sangara, in the Anzourou region inland from the left bank and near the Mali border; in the Hombori mountains region of eastern Mali; in Arham and Tendirma, farther north; and in Aribinda, in eastern Burkina Faso not far from the Niger border.

225–30   The daughter who becomes a *sorko* also appears today as the mother of all future *sorkos*.

231   Here the griot clearly distinguishes between the *sorkos* and ordinary hunters by saying that they are not simply *gawaye*, or hunters who happened to work in the water, but are in fact more than that, they are both fishermen and people endowed with special powers. Olivier de Sardan points out that there are two kinds of *sorko*—master fishermen descended from Faran Maka Bote who play the role of griots for the Tooru family of spirits, and who are the only ones who may hunt hippopotamuses, and ordinary fishermen who live upstream from Timbuktu. While he adds that the *Taríkh el-Fettâch* lists the Sorko among the servile tribes of Mali who were liberated by Sonni Ali Ber, he also points out that the citation (*TF* 107) comes from the section that some scholars, in particular Levtzion, have attributed to Sékou Amadou in the nineteenth century (1982, 342–43).

238   "Converted" means that he changed them to the Islamic faith.

271   The Mossi are not on the direct path to Mecca but live southwest of Gao. Here the griot seems to be conflating two events: first the view, reported in both the oral and written accounts, of the Mossi as nonbelievers in Islam, and second, the pilgrimage to Mecca.

278   Liboré is a canton seat 12 kilometers downriver from Saga.

291   The use of "horses" to indicate cavaliers here is an example of metonymy that appears frequently later on. Only by the context can it be determined that not only the animals are referred to here.

306   Modi Baja appears as both a proper name and as a more recent term for a type of marabout whose strength lies in divination. *Modibo* is the Fulani term for marabout. Today, according to Diouldé Laya, the word *moodibaajo* means a person of Fulani origin who is a marabout.

334   This line marks the place where Nouhou Malio used gesture for the only time during his performance. While sitting in his chair, he thrust his hands down between his knees to the floor to show how Askia Mohammed grabbed the plants growing at the bottom of the hole.

340–41   At this point, Nouhou Malio breaks out into loud laughter at the contrasting images of the griots' ancestor, who was so improvident as to eat the plants, and that of Modi Baja, who was careful to bring some home. Nouhou Malio's explanation that this event is the

.. why griots must suffer to earn their livelihood is one of many ..erent etiological tales about griots one can find in the Sahel today.

347–73   Here we find a praise poem from the past for Askia Mohammed that includes Soninké terms. The readings of "Long live" from *dallay* (ll. 347–48), and "proceeded" from *suliyan* (l. 350) were provided by Papa Bunka Susso, a Mandinka griot from eastern Gambia who grew up in a Soninké village and who considers Soninké as a second maternal language (interview February 17, 1988). *Mamadi* is the Soninké diminutif for "Mohammed."

352   The Indigo Tree is an ancient term for the Kaaba, the shrine of Islam at Mecca. It is always covered with tapestries. Seen from a distance, it appears in the sun as indigo. Line 349 contains a Soninké term *jiido*, which, according to Papa Susso, means "many trees."

357–358   The original Songhay refers to Yabilan. Two sources suggest that the term refers to Dongo, the Songhay god of thunder and lightning. Stoller has reported to me that Yabilan is the term used by healers and magicians in their incantations to refer to Dongo. Oumarou Watta, in a conversation with me on August 30, 1988, suggested that the term combines *ya*, "to call," as in a listing of ancestors, and *bilan*, a term for Dongo. In either case, the reference to a Songhay deity invoked for protection on the way to Mecca underscores the significance of the traditional system of beliefs even at the hero's moment of greatest involvement in Islam.

388   The singular term "horse" here, from *bariyo*, is a singular form of metonymy for a plural noun, cavalry. On some occasions the griot uses the literal term for cavalier, *barikaro*. I have translated *bariyo* literally as "horse" and leave it to the reader to determine the figurative meaning from the context. One possible reason for the metonymic link between horses and men is the high value placed on horses. Kimba, citing a French officer named Baudry, reports that at the end of the nineteenth century, a horse was worth from two to five slaves; another of his sources indicated that at the beginning of the twentieth century, a horse was worth from five to ten slaves. In addition to the relatively high cost of horses, notes Kimba, the animals require careful and costly maintenance (1981, 64).

385   Nouhou Malio uses an elliptical style here that does not conform to normal usage. The line should be followed by either *do* or *ra* to indicate "place of" or "among."

395   "What time" here comes from *ler fo*, an anachronism made up of a French word, *heure* ("hour" in English) and a Songhay interrogative pronoun, *ifo*, which means "what."

403–04   The frequent references to the Bargantché here lead the griot to make an apparent slip of the tongue by terming the *sohanci* a Bargantché—unless the *sohanci* happened to be of Bargantché origin. There is also an apparent confusion here when he says that the man first went out of the village and then adds in the following line that he went away from the crowd—unless the crowd happened to be outside of the village in the first place.

407–08   The comparison of the speed of the flying *sohanci* with that of an airplane is the first reference to the technology of Western civilization in the narrative. The following line provides an African comparison with the image of a hawk.

409   Sikiyay, listed as Sikyé, is a small village on the right bank of the Niger between Boubon and Karma, 20 kilometers upriver from Niamey near Namaro. According to Olivier de Sardan, citing Larue, it is the last place or residence of the *askias* (1982, 329–30). Streicker, referring to "a certain body of legends" apparently mentioned by French historians Jean Périe and Michel Sellier, explains that there was a seventeenth-century chief named Sikia, who is said to have lived at the village of Sikiey on the banks of the Niger. "'Sikia' is undoubtedly a deformation of the Songhay 'askia' and the term probably refers to one or a succession of the minor askias installed at Sikiey, in Dendi during the seventeenth century" (Streicker 1980, 105).

410   This is the first reference to Askia Mohammed's wife. From a subsequent reference on line 477 to marriage between Askia Mohammed and the Songhay, it would appear that Sana, like her husband, was not of Songhay origin.

413–16   There is some confusion here about who is talking. From the text, it appears first that the *sohanci* travels alone. But when he lands, the dialogue between him and the people of Sikiyay is conducted in the plural form, as if the *sohanci* had come with an entourage. But on lines 422–25, the *sohanci* reverts to speech in the singular as he gives instructions for the naming of the child. Throughout this encounter, it seems surprising that the *sohanci*, Askia Mohammed's envoy, does not know his leader's wife (l. 415). This lack of knowledge might be explained by the fact that Askia Mo-

...d had wives in many, many areas where he traveled. It could be the griot's way of raising and then answering a question for his listeners.

422–25   In the sequence of lines where the *sohanci* gives instructions for naming, there appears to be an inconsistency in chronology. On line 424, the *sohanci* reports that the child has been given a name, but on 425 either he or the narrator announced that he should be given the name of Daouda.

426   The Daouda in question here is most likely the man who became Askia Daoud. He ruled as an energetic and enlightened leader during the middle of the sixteenth century.

430–31   The *sohanci's* flight pattern evidently took him straight up the Niger River valley, for after Sikiyay, he arrives at the home of Kassaye in Gao.

477–78   The notion of marriage here implies a pact between two different peoples—in this case the ruler of foreign origin and the Songhay people. Instead of using the usual term for marriage, *hiiji*, the griot uses a more formal expression, *tirahaw*, a term that means "to celebrate a marriage" according to Olivier de Sardan (1982, 354). But he points out that the literal meaning is "to attach the Book," a definition with multiple connotations here. It refers to a religious benediction in the form of a public prayer, *alfatiya*, that a marabout pronounces at the moment two families agree on the dowry. Thus Askia Mohammed, having made the pilgrimage to Mecca, seeks to confirm his relationship with the Songhay in the way that reflects most appropriately his status as a defender of Islam. Later (l. 1138) we shall see the term used again by Sagouma to seal a relationship with the enemy in order to take revenge against Soumayla Kassa, her former husband, who has violated just such a pact by killing her brother.

The following line, referring to different marriage customs adopted since the arrival of Europeans in Africa, does not seem directly related to the preceding line, but appears instead to be simply the griot's comment on how marriage customs have changed from the old days when they were much simpler.

481   The news that his first child fathered in the Songhay area is Moussa Zara seems to contradict the earlier birth of Daouda. One might conclude that Moussa Zara was his first child fathered since the formal marriage pact with the Songhay described a few lines earlier.

But the Gobir region, home of Moussa's mother, lies 450 kilometers east of Niamey and is part of a Hausaphone region that Askia Mohammed did not conquer until after his return from Mecca (1506–13, according to Boubou Hama). Hama does, nevertheless, report in his *Histoire du Gobir et de Sokoto* (1967) that inhabitants of the Gobir region were closely linked to the Songhay and Zarma many centuries ago.

The Moussa in question was evidently the son who forced Askia Mohammed out of office, but this is not clear from the oral narrative. Later, at lines 641–82, the griot returns to Moussa Zara in more detail, in order, it seems, to review and expand on what he had said about this ruler during the first taping session.

483   The name "Almanyauri" is the Soninké version of "Moussa," according to Fatima Mounkaila (interview with the author, September 13, 1989).

491   Mohamma Gao here may refer to Askia Mohammed Gao, the man who overthrew Askia Ishâq II after the retreat from Tondibi to Gao. But the context is too ambiguous to make a positive identification.

497   The reference to Isaka is not clear, but the metaphors associated with him suggest a man of great strength and force, with his own ideas.

499   The Si in this otherwise undecipherable line may be Sonni Ali Ber.

508   The story that begins here about Daouda killing the lions appears in many versions and is undoubtedly a very old text, judging from the high percentage of undecipherable lines. Some of it is obviously Soninké, but even those who know the language cannot decipher the text.

544   I have been unable to identify Gombo. In his own Songhay recounting of the story of Daouda, Boubou Hama's narrator says that Daouda goes out on the road to Timbuktu (1969, 51).

570   *Baabayzey* in the narrowest sense means children of the same father but of different mothers, so I have translated it here as half brothers. But in a broader sense it refers to the larger community of brothers and cousins who may all claim, directly or indirectly, a share in the *baabayzey faada*, or "house of the father."

586   The first "they" in the line refers to Daouda's half brothers, while the second appears to mean that both Daouda and his horse

fought as a team to kill the lions.

591–610   The metaphoric image of Daouda as Namaro here means that he settled there and its people descend from him. Namaro is 45 kilometers upriver from Niamey on the right bank. The griot points out later (ll. 611–12) that the people of Karma, a few kilometers downstream on the left bank, also come from the same lineage.

598   The literal reading of this name is "Mamadou Thin Neck": *Djinde Marria*. The same family name is applied to several other descendants of Daouda on lines 599, 604, and 605.

608–9   The term *sorkayze* as part of names in these two lines means "son of a *sorko*."

609   This marks the last line of the performance on December 30, 1980. The following line is the first line of the performance on January 26, 1981. Four weeks elapsed between recordings because Nouhou Malio was ill. Before beginning the second performance, he listened to the end of the first recording.

625–83   Nouhou Malio repeats praises here for Mamar and Daouda, including those recounting the trip to Mecca, and the metaphoric descriptions of Moussa Zara.

637, 791, 799   It is not clear here if *Bodronkou* is a person or if it is the Soninké term for Songhay, as Fatima Mounkaila has suggested (interview with the author, September 10, 1989). Boubé Gado, citing the late griot Badié Bagna, reports that the expression *Bodorinko si Gao* is Soninké. *Bodorinko, Bodorinke,* and *Bodoro,* according to this interpretation, would be Soninké terms for the Songhay. Gado, drawing on Cuoq (1975), asks if these terms come from "al-Bozorganiyn," the word for the inhabitants of ancient Gao according to al-Bekri. If it is the latter, then the lines would mean that it is in one place that Askia Mohammed began to father Songhay descendants (1980, 146).

639   Zara Minyauri is a variant of Almanyauri.

644–678   The meaning of this series of metaphors is simply that nobody can touch Moussa Zara, in particular his half brothers born of the same father, Askia Mohammed, but of different mothers. The kind of fraternal rivalry expressed in this passage appears throughout the Sahel and in many other areas of the world where polygamy is practiced.

714   This line means that if you strike a stone, you wound yourself in the process.

735   The name "Harigoni" means "expert swimmer."

742   The name "Yerima" means "lieutenant."

749   Yéni is a town 90 kilometers east of Niamey and 40 kilometers north of Dosso in the Boboye Valley.

758   Sansane-Haoussa is a small town 60 kilometers north of Niamey on the left bank.

762   The expression *haw sambu* is ambiguous here. Together the two words can mean "spot the scent;" "haw" alone can mean "wind" or "cow," depending on the pronunciation.

776   Komdiago here probably refers to Askia Mohammed's brother and his descendants.

787   The literal "was called" here means "was descended from."

804   The Kassa here, mother of Soumayla, is not the same one who was Askia Mohammed's mother, not only because Soumayla, in both the written and oral versions, rules long after the death of Askia Mohammed, but also because her name is slightly different—Kassa versus Kassaye—from that of the first woman in the narrative. In Songhay, Kassa means "a woman who is coddled."

818   There is no indication when he ruled Gao, but from other evidence, it is likely that he held the chieftaincy there toward the end of Moroccan hegemony in the region, between 1630 and 1640.

855   It is difficult to follow the narrative shifts here from descriptions of Amar Zoumbani, referred to by his supporters as "our prince," to the real prince, "The brother of Sagouma, who is the son of the former chief" (l. 864). At certain points, I have simply inferred the difference by listening to the tape.

869   *Yalli* here is not a Songhay word. It appears to come from the Soninké *yalla*, to stroll about.

883   "This so-and-so" appears here not as an insult but as a form of indirect address typical of the widespread tendency toward indirection in Songhay speech. For example, a wife will never call her husband by his first name.

942   The term *zaago* here is not entirely clear. It is either a technical term in Songhay for a particular type of horse or a word borrowed from another language.

960, 981   The term "prayer ground" here is translated from *bon giso do*, literally "the place where one puts one's head down," rather than from the usual term, *iddo do*.

1014   Amar's immediate sadness stems from the trickery of his father's servants, and it is this that provokes his father to seek to remedy the larger concern, that caused by the insulting gesture of Sagouma's brother who gave Soumayla Kassa's son to the griots.

1038   "Whoops" is an approximate translation of the ideophone *urufo* to represent the sudden movement of falling.

1046   "Window" here comes from the transformation of the French term *fenêtre* into *finetro*, and refers not to glass windows but to square or round holes in mud-walled houses.

1049   "Artisan" here comes from *garassa* and refers probably to leatherworker, although if used for men it normally means blacksmith, according to Olivier de Sardan. He reports that *garassa* means today Tuareg craftsman, a term that includes not only the notion of artisan but also that of griot. The origin of the term in the Songhay world remains unclear, but it has been linked to the Mandé term *garance*, leatherworker, as well as to the ancient, pre-Songhay Gara (Garamantes) who worked iron (1982, 155–56). On line 1074, the griot uses another term, *konnya*, to indicate that the woman is of captive origin. The Tuareg *garassa* was free, but in this particular context it is clear that the *garassa* is of captive origin.

1057   "Out with it" is a rough translation of an onomatopoeic expression *urururu*, which has the negative connotatons of excretion. In the same line, *garaasio* could be translated as either "little artisan" or "little griot." In this context, however, little griot, or the feminine form for griot, *griotte*, conveys best Sagouma's exasperation and condescending manner.

1066   The *godji* (also spelled *godje*) is a monocord violin made of a calabash about thirty centimeters in diameter covered with the skin of *Varanus niloticus*, a type of large lizard, and fitted with a wood neck about sixty centimeters long and a string made of horsehair. For the Songhay and Zarma, the instrument serves in a variety of religious ceremonies, especially possession ceremonies such as the *yenendi*, to call forth those spirits, or *tooru*, who will bring rain. Bernard Surugue reports that many peoples in the Sahel use similar instruments, among them the Hausa, the Tuareg, the Gourmantché, the Wolof, the Mossi, and others (1972, 8). In this context, the fact that Sagouma plays the *godji* "for singing to princes" suggests that the instrument is used for entertainment purposes, not for a particular ritual. Nevertheless, given the significance of the *godji* for possession dances, *yenendi*, and other ceremonies, it is hard not to attach some greater spiritual significance to the woman who plays it here. Stoller explains that "the godji's sound links the Songhay present and past. Its wailing reinforces deep-seated cultural themes about the nature of life and death, the origin of the Songhay, and the juxtaposition of the social and spirit worlds" (1989, 112).

1079–83   Sagouma's killing of her two sons represents more than simply a double infanticide. It is the revenge of one family on another for the violation of a pact.

1089   *Arma* here is a derivation from *rumāt*, an Arabic word for soldiers carrying firearms (Saad 1983, 297), and refers either to the soldiers who were part of the Moroccan-directed army of conquest or to their descendants who participated in a series of increasingly fruitless campaigns during the next few generations to maintain Moroccan control over the region. The ambiguity stems from the term *armahalley* used by the griot. Olivier de Sardan's sources distinguish between the *almahalle*, or so-called Moroccans who conquered the region, and the *arma* who were their sixteenth- and seventeenth-century descendants. If the battle described in the narrative is the fall of Gao, then the *armahalley* used by Nouhou Malio to designate the aggressors could be translated most appropriately as either "Moroccans," with quotation marks to indicate not simply Moroccans, but also Andalusians and men from other areas who signed up for the expedition, or as Arma, to indicate the descendants who, half a century after the conquest, fought unsuccessfully against a rebellious Gao. Given the griot's conflation of both events, the term *Arma* appears to reflect most accurately the historical reality behind the oral text (1982, 27–28, 35–36).

1100   "Bull," from the term *bardo*, refers to the bull that one sacrifices at a wedding and, by extension, all the expenses incurred for the ceremony.

1107   "Passes you by" is the griot's way of putting the listener in the place of the man who cannot meet Sagouma's requirements.

1112   Literally, "I come to be the stranger."

1138   Here again, the notion of marriage takes on a more legal sense with the use of the term *tirahaw* rather than the simpler *hiiji* to indicate a social tie.

1164   The comparison between early Songhay forms of government and today appears in the use of the term *gufernema* from the French to signify "government."

1187, 1192 The reference to the contributions of the rich to Bayero's war fund may be interpreted in at least two ways: (1) wars cost money, and one cannot conduct a war without the support of the rich; and (2) the rich sold out to the Moroccans in exchange for economic peace. The following lines, however, which report the involvement of marabouts and women, suggest that the griot seeks to emphasize widespread support for Bayero's effort against Gao.

1204 The reference to the role of women as suppliers appears to underscore the dependence of men on women in the conduct of a war. The griot points out that both men and their animals rely on the ability of women to keep the supplies flowing toward the front line at Gao.

1221 The "It" refers to the army of Bayero. "Their" refers to the people of Gao.

1233–59 The chicken does not bring to mind any particular link with the Songhay belief system, except that it is a common object of sacrifice in ceremonies. But the python and the ox offer a variety of interpretations from both the local and the broader Sahelian context.

The snake is an important symbol of power as least as far back as the Ghana empire with the myth of the serpent called Bida. The McIntoshes found a variety of snake motifs in pottery at Jenne-Jeno, the site of a city near the modern Malian city of Djenné that dates back to 250 B.C. (1982). In an extended discussion of the role of snakes among various peoples, Boubou Hama (1966) notes that among the Songhay of the Téra region, there still exist serpent cults in the watercourses that lead to the Niger River (139–68). Snakes are found among the *gengi bi*, one of the five families of Songhay spirits, reports Stoller. He describes the appearance of a person possessed by a snake during the ritual sacrifice of animals marking the sixth day of a seven-day initiation of a woman as a medium in the Songhay spirit world (1989, 69–70). Daouda Sorko, a Nigérien keeper of the oral tradition, reported to archaeologist Boubé Gado that the killer of Ghana Empire's Bida snake was Mali Keyna, younger brother of Mali Bero (Mounkaila 1985, 210). Whether or not the appearance here of a snake as one of the protective spirits of Gao has any relation to the Bida snake—for example, through the Soninké language connection—remains to be documented. From the context, Diouldé Laya suggests that there is probably some sort of connection (marginal notes to draft of this manuscript and interviews with the author, Niamey, February 1989).

As for the ox, there is a tradition among the Zarma people that their ancestors were guided to their current location in Niger by a bull. The animal is the sacred bull of Dongo, Songhay-Zarma deity of thunder and lightning (see Mounkaila 1985, 248).

1262   *Dili* is a game played with small pebbles or seeds and a board with twelve holes common to many parts of Africa.

1269–72   The word for woman is *weyboro* in Songhay. The griot's shortening of *wandiya jeyante* or "older, unmarried woman" (l. 1269) to simply *wandiya* or "girl" in lines 1270 and 1272 creates a translation problem—how can the person be a woman and then a girl? I have resolved the ambiguity simply by placing "girl" in quotation marks to indicate that she is really much older than a girl.

1323–54   Sagouma's advice to her Arma friend to stay away from Soumayla Kassa seems to contradict her earlier wish for a man who can kill her former husband. The fact that she begins to play the *godji*, and that the music and praises attracts her husband, almost as a magic charm, invites at least two interpretations: (1) She wants to give Bayero a chance to prove himself; (2) she wants to prove to Bayero the truth of her words about Soumayla's prowess.

1390   The kokorbey (*Combretum glutinosum*) is a type of tree common to the Sahel. It ranges from five to seventeen meters tall and its bark is used in powdered form to treat stomach pains.

1411   Fifty thousand CFA francs equaled $150 at the time of the performance but is now worth $100.

1425   "Secret" here is an approximate translation of *genji haw* which Stoller defines literally as "to attach or tie up the bush"; this is the most important incantation in a sorcerer's repertoire—its aim is to harmonize the forces of the bush (1989, 232).

1431–32   The belief that there is danger in going into town and fraternizing with the local people, particularly the women, is hardly new in the history of warfare. Here, however, there is some confusion about the causes of what appears to be a temporary setback (l. 1448) for the Songhay. The village near which Soumayla Kassa, Amar Zoumbani, and their soldiers stop appears to be a friendly one. But Amar Zoumbani compounds his error in sleeping with a local woman by violating a taboo against getting on and off a horse in the morning when he requests a change in saddles (ll. 1427–28, 1441). The significance of the incident seems to be that Amar Zoumbani's acts manifest, once again, the captive side of his mixed noble/captive heritage.

1449–54   The report that the Songhay cavalry kill all the Arma horses or horsemen implies that the Songhay were turning the tide in their resistance against the Arma. In this passage, following previous usage, the context would seem to suggest that the enemy cavalry were killed, rather than the horses themselves. But here the griot distinguishes between the Songhay cavalry, using the unambiguous term *barikaro*, and the enemy, which he describes as horses, or *bariyey*.

1457   One can still visit the grave of Mali Bero at the village of Sargan, 7 kilometers south of Ouallam, a provincial capital of the Zarmaganda region 75 kilometers north of Niamey.

1533   "How awful" here comes from a Soninké term for death, *kaari*, according to Papa Susso. But in Songhay, it is simply a very strong epithet to express surprise and concern. Interview, Harouna Beidari and Idrissa Souley, Karma, February 11, 1989.

1539   Mali understands the language of the horses and wants to see if the Fulani seer has heard the same news.

1548   The harangue by Yefarma here reflects the philosophy of the warrior who fights for his commander-in-chief, or *wangu nya*, literally "mother of the science of war" (Ousmane Mahamane Tandina 1984 and interviews with the author, October 1987; Boubé Gado 1980, 240–43).

1555   The reference to "A man" here is an indirect way of referring to the self (Dioulbé Laya, marginal note to draft of this manuscript, February 1989).

1582   The term *koba* here refers no doubt to the kobe tree, *Ficus platyphylla*. Stoller reports that its bark is ground into a powder and used in sorcery and medecine for a variety of purposes (interview with the author, August 20, 1989).

1589   *Hasagay* is an ambiguous term here. According to Papa Susso (interviews with the author, February 1988), it means "lucky" in Soninké. Manthia Diawara, an ethnic Soninké, suggests that it means here simply "special" or "magic" to signify the link between that part of the body of either man or animal and the Gollé people (interviews with the author, March 1988). In interviews at Saga in April 1988, Soumana Abdou, Nouhou Malio's accompanist, reported to Ousmane Mahamane Tandina that the term refers to the meat of an animal that has been killed for a celebration (for example, a naming ceremony) and indicates more specifically the part of the animal reserved for a particu-

lar ethnic group—in this case the Gollé. He adds that the leg is reserved for the griot. Harouna Beidari and Idrissa Souley, griots,
explained that it refers to meat from the chest of an animal (Karma,
February 11, 1989).

1602 Kourfeye (also spelled Kurfey) is a region 90 kilometers
southeast of Boubon in the Dallol Bosso area. According to French
geographer Yveline Poncet, the Kourfeye people today originally came
from Bornou, far to the east, but arrived there after the Zarma Kallé,
cousins of the Gollé (1973, 24).

BIBLIOGRAPHY

Ba, Adam Konare. *Sonni Ali Ber*. Niamey: Institut de Recherches en Sciences Humaines, 1977.

Cissoko, Sékéné Mody. *Tombouctou et l'Empire Songhay*. Dakar: Nouvelles Editions Africaines, 1975.

Conrad, David C., and Barbara E. Frank, eds. *Status and Identity in West Africa: Nyamakalaw of Mande*. Bloomington: Indiana University Press, 1995.

Cuoq, Joseph. *Histoire de l'islamisation de l'Afrique de l'Ouest*. Paris: Centre National de la Recherche Scientifique, 1984.

Hale, Thomas A. *Scribe, Griot, and Novelist: Narrative Interpreters of the Songhay Empire. Followed by the Epic of Askia Mohammed Recounted by Nouhou Malio*. Gainesville: University of Florida Press, 1990.

——, writer and producer, and Marie Hornbein, director and editor. *Griottes of the Sahel: Female Keepers of the Oral Tradition in Niger*, 11-minute video. Center for Instructional Design and Interactive Technologies, Pennsylvania State University, 1990. Distributed by Audio-Visual Services, The Pennsylvania State University.

Hama, Boubou. *Histoire du Gobir et du Sokoto*. Paris: Présence Africaine, 1967.

——. *Histoire des Songhay*. Paris: Présence Africaine, 1968.

——. *Manta Mantaari*. N.p., 1969.

Hunwick, John O. *Shari'a in Songhay: The Replies of Al-Maghili to the Questions of Askia Al-Hajj Muhammad*. Oxford: Oxford University Press, 1985.

Johnson, John William, and Fa-Digi Sisòkò. *The Epic of Son-Jara: A West African Tradition*. Bloomington: Indiana University Press, 1992.

Karl, Emmanuel. *Traditions orales au Dahomey-Benin*. Niamey: Centre Régional de Documentation pour la Tradition Orale, 1974.

Kâti, Mahmoud. *Tarîkh el-Fettâch ou chronique du chercheur pour servir à l'histoire des villes, des armées et des principaux personnages du Tekrour*. Trans. O. Houdas and M. Delafosse. Paris: Ernest Leroux, 1913.

Kimba, Idrissa. *Guerres et sociétés: les populations du "Niger" occidental au XIXe siècle et leurs réactions face à la colonisation (1896–1906)*. Niamey: Institut de Recherches en Sciences Humaines, 1981.

McIntosh, Susan Keech, and Roderick J. "Finding Jenne-Jeno, West Africa's Oldest City." *National Geographic* 162, no. 3 (1982): 396–418.

Mounkaila, Fatima. "Le Mythe et l'histoire dans le geste de Zabarkane." Diss., University of Dakar, 1985. Published as *Mythe et Histoire dans la geste de*

Zabarkane. Niamey: Centre d'Etudes Linguistique et Historique par Tradition Orale, 1989.

Olivier de Sardan, Jean-Pierre. *Concepts et Conceptions songhay-zarma.* Paris: Nubia, 1982.

———. *Les sociétés songhay-zarma (Niger - Mali): chefs, querriers, esclaves, paysans . . .* Paris: Karthala, 1984.

Poncet, Yveline. *Cartes ethno-démographiques du Niger au 1/1,000,000.* Niamey: Centre Nigérien de Recherches en Sciences Humaines, 1973.

Rouch, Jean. *La religion et la magie songhay.* Brussels: Editions de l'Université de Bruxelles. 2nd edition. 1989.

Saad, Elias. *Social History of Timbuktu.* Cambridge: Cambridge University Press, 1983.

Stoller, Paul. *The Cinematic Griot: The Ethnography of Jean Rouch.* Chicago: University of Chicago Press, 1992.

———. *Fusion of the Worlds: An Ethnography of Possession among the Songhay of Niger.* Chicago: University of Chicago Press, 1989.

———. *The Taste of Things Ethnographic: The Senses in Anthropology.* Philadelphia: University of Pennsylvania Press, 1989.

Stoller, Paul, and Cheryl Olkes. *In Sorcery's Shadow: A Memoir of an Apprenticeship among the Songhay of Niger.* Chicago: University of Chicago Press, 1987.

Surugue, Bernard. *Contribution à l'étude de la musique sacrée zarma songhay.* Niamey: Centre Nigérien de Recherches en Sciences Humaines, 1972.

Tandina, Ousmane Mahamane. "Une épopée zarma: Wangougna Issa Korombeïze Modi ou Issa Koygolo, 'Mère de la science de la guerre.'" Diss., University of Dakar, 1984.

INDEX

THOMAS A. HALE is a Professor of African, French, and Comparative Literature at The Pennsylvania State University. He is the author of *Scribe, Griot, and Novelist* and *Les Ecrits d'Aimé Césaire*, as well as co-editor, with Richard K. Priebe, of *The Teaching of African Literature* and *Artist and Audience: African Literature as a Shared Experience*.